Charles Craig Lantz, ThD,

G000166355

APOLOGETICS MADE SIMPLE

3 ESSAYS FOR BEGINNERS

BY

Charles Craig Lantz, ThD, PhD

February 2019

Sophia's House Publications

Ovid, Michigan

USA

Charles Craig Lantz, ThD, PhD

THE NEED FOR APOLOGETICS IN AN AGE OF SKEPTICISM

"Is God willing to prevent evil, but not able? Then he is not omnipotent. Is he able, but not willing? Then he is malevolent. Is he both able and willing? Then whence cometh evil? Is he neither able nor willing? Then why call him God?" -- **Epicurus**

"Men never do evil so completely and cheerfully as when they do it from religious conviction." -- **Blaise Pascal**

"Question: How do you know you're God?
Answer: Simple. When I pray to him, I find I'm talking to myself." -- **Peter O'Toole**

"I am against religion because it teaches us to be satisfied with not understanding the world." -- **Richard Dawkins**

"The essence of Christianity is told us in the Garden of Eden history. The fruit that was forbidden was on the tree of knowledge. The subtext is, All the suffering you have is because you wanted to find out what was going on." -- **Frank Zappa**

"One's convictions should be proportional to one's evidence." -- **Sam Harris**

Charles Craig Lantz, ThD, PhD

This book is dedicated to those who, according to Jude,

"fight earnestly for the faith"

"Beloved, while I was very diligent to write to you concerning our common salvation, I found it necessary to write to you exhorting you to contend earnestly for **the faith** which was once for all delivered to the saints."

Jude 3 (NKJV)

Charles Craig Lantz, ThD, PhD

TABLE OF CONTENTS

Charles Craig Lantz, ThD, PhD

CHAPTER ONE

APOLOGETICS I: A BASIC FOUNDATION

Agnosticism[1]

The concept of "agnosticism" basically means that one is not sure whether or not God exist. There are basically two types of agnostics: there are those that claim that God is simply "unknowable" and those that claim the existence of God, and his nature, are simply not known. The leading proponents of agnosticism historically are David Hume, Immanuel Kant, and A.J. Ayer. For these philosophers there is simply no basis for making any true statements about

---

1 The primary source of information found in this chapter is from the book, *Christian Apologetics,* by Dr. Norman Geisler. He is considered one of the top philosophers and Christian Apologist in the world, he has authored over 35 books. See **Christian Apologetics** by Norman Geisler, Ph.D., Baker Book House: Grand Rapids, Michigan, Third Printing—March 2006.

God. For them, God simply cannot be known by any rational or empirically measured data to verify His existence. If there is a God, He is simply "unknowable."

Agnosticism is proven to be self-defeating upon examination. Simply put, the skepticism of agnosticism reduces all meaning down to this self-defeating statement: "One knows enough about reality in order to affirm that nothing can be known about reality" (Geisler 2006, 20). This statement in itself is self-defeating because one cannot know "something" about reality, yet, in the same breath say that all of reality is "unknowable." This statement is the essential non-sense and self-defeating logic of these philosophers surveyed, for these type of statements defeat themselves for this reason: the argument assumes some knowledge about reality in order to deny any solid knowable knowledge of "reality." This is the basic problem that these philosophers face.

Another example of this is the principle of A.J. Ayer that all knowledge of reality must be empirically verifiable, which is also self-defeating. To make a claim that there is "nothing" of reality that can be known unless it can be proven scientifically is simply not a rational claim. To claim that "nothing" about reality can be proven is to claim that "something" about reality exists, namely, that nothing exists. This is a self-defeating claim; it is comparable to the modern skeptic who says, "There are NO ABSOLUTES." That person just made an ABSOLUTE STATEMENT: *THAT THERE ARE NO ABSOLUTES!* This type of reasoning is circular, self-contradictory, and contains self-defeating statements that simply will not hold up to logic and examination. This is the basic view of agnosticism.

Rationalism

Rationalism is "characterized by its stress on the innate or *a priori* ability of human reason to know truth" (Ibid., 29). This means that knowledge of truth is possible independent of human experience, Viz., *a priori*.[1] Rationalist

---

1 A PRIORI- means relating to or denoting reasoning or knowledge which proceeds from theoretical deduction rather than from observation of human experience. An example would be: "She made an a priori assumption about human nature."

believe that truth is knowable or demonstrable by human reason alone independent of human experience or sensory perception. In modern times, the three main proponents of rationalism are Rene Descartes (1596-1650), Benedict Spinoza (1632-1677), and Gottfried Leibniz (1646-1716). These philosophers all argued for God's existence through the use of human reason, logic and deductive arguments, such as the ontological argument for God's existence.

The basic idea of this argument is that because we have an idea of a perfect God, it must necessitate that there is in actuality a perfect God, because, it would be impossible to have such a notion as to imagine it without it being actually possible. The problem with this type of rationality is that just because one can think of the Easter Bunny, that is perfect, does not mean in actuality that the Easter Bunny does in fact exist. Just because someone has a thought about a beings possible existence, does not prove its existence, and this is the weakness of rationalism.

Hence, Geisler says, "it is based on an invalid move

from thought to reality, from the possible to the actual. The thinkable describes only the realm of the possible and not necessarily that of the actual" (Ibid., 42). Essentially, it is not possible to prove God's existence through the use of logic and reason alone. This is the failure of the rationalist philosophy.

Fideism

Fideism is the belief that one cannot use reason to find truth. For the fideist, truth in matters of religion rests solely on ones "faith" and not on the human mental process of reasoning. There are at least four great fideism thinkers that are proponents of this view: **Blaise Pascal** (1623-1662), **Soren Kierkegaard** (1813-1855), **Karl Barth,** and the late **Cornelius Van Til**. We will briefly examine the views of Pascal and Kierkegaard in this section. According to Geisler, "Pascal desired to destroy faith in reason so that he could restore 'faith in faith'" (Ibid., 48). Pascal was convinced that true saving faith was an issue of the heart, not the head (reason). For him, it is the heart of man that experiences God not the pure intellect of man or his reasoning process.

Faith is a gift from God that is given to us so that we can believe and place our human trust in a personal being, not in our reasoning process. Pascal is certain that one must accept or reject God's truth by faith and not reason. Pascal is best known for his great "wager" or bet on the existence of God. For Pascal, the best bet is to believe in God's existence. If He does exist and you choose to believe, then, you will ultimately gain everything and lose nothing. If, however, God does not exist, and you still choose to believe, you still lose nothing. Finally, if God does exist, and one chooses to not believe or wager on God's existence, then, in the final analysis, one would lose eternal life and lose everything. This is Pascal's famous "wager" or bet on God's existence.

Another great thinker and fideist, that will be surveyed in this section is Soren Kierkegaard. For him, one must take a giant "blind leap of faith", a non-rational leap into faith in God. The blind leap is a decision of the will that is not an irrational decision, but, is one that is simply "non-rational." For Kierkegaard, "Faith is man's highest passion" (Ibid., 52). True faith is a submission of the will to God through Jesus Christ, it is subjective, not objective. A person responds to God as an act of their will when confronted with God. Essentially, according to Kierkegaard, faith is an act of the will that has no use for reasoning, for God reveals Himself and one connects with God by faith-not intellect.

Once God has revealed Himself to a person, one must respond to God by faith- this is the blind leap, this is the will making a decision to choose God, this is not something that is forced upon us. "Faith in God is neither rationally nor empirically grounded; so the existence of God is neither rationally certain nor empirically evident" (Ibid., 52). In Summary, Kierkegaard believed that faith, not reason, is the path or doorway to the truth. This form of fideism is not irrational; rather, it is simply a "non-rational" leap into God, existentially reached by faith.

The main weakness of fideism is that it provides a position that is inadequate since it is not a plausible explanation for testing truth claims. Moreover, other people have beliefs that are contrary to Christianity. For example, some people believe that Martians are our savior, which is simply not true. Fideism fails to give us an adequate test objectively for what is truth, or what is *being believed* by fideist. This, then, is the basic explanation of the beliefs of philosophers known as fideism.

Experientialism

Experientialism is the belief that "experience" is the final court of appeals in terms of what is known as "truth." When one has the personal experience of God in their conscious state of being, then, one has the final test for truth, according to the proponents of this view. This is the basic premise or thesis of the "experientialist." An example of a proponent of this view is that of Plotinus. He was a Pantheistic Mystic who believed, as did his followers, that "God cannot be known for he is literally the Unknowable;

God can only be felt or intuited by mystical union" (Ibid., 67). For Plotinus, experiences with God are not knowable, which means that it can't be defined with words because they are inexpressible. The experience of God is in essence the "proof" of its truth. There is no reason or evidence given to define truth; it is simply a subjective experience with God.

Friedrich Schleiermacher (1768-1834) is another thinker and proponent of experientialism. For him the personal experience of God is the main thing to be concerned with as a primary focus; while religious thought process is a later reflection of the spiritual experience one has had with God. Geisler summarizes his view, "Ethics is a way of living, science is a way of thinking, but religion is a way of feeling. It is not just any way of feeling but it is the feeling of being utterly dependent on the All" (Ibid., 69).

Schleiermacher also believed in the religious intuition in man. For him the essence of religion is God operating on the soul of man which produces a feeling of piety; religious feelings as such cannot be taught, rather, they must be caught. Religious intuition is the sum of all "higher feelings" according to Schleiermacher. "This inner feeling of the universe makes us whole and unified. Dogmas are formed as a result of reflection on this feeling. Dogmas are not necessary for religious life and aid little in the communication of it" (Ibid., 71).

As an evaluation of experientialism, it is noteworthy at least for three different reasons: (1) Experience is essential to the foundation of which all truth is built; (2) in a broad and general sense, experience is the final court of appeals, in that, even when one uses human reasoning and rational thought, that too is an "experience"; and finally, (3) primary experience is the ground or foundation for the secondary experiences. In other words, what we believe and affirm grows out of our experiences with God; not the other way around.

Negatively, there are at least three difficulties with Experientialism. First, experience as such is neither true nor false, it just is. A person has an experience, and the truth is something one expresses about the experience. Once a person has an experience, then, the person will test whether or not it is true based upon thought and proper evaluation. Secondly, experience alone can't be used to prove or support the truth of that experience, for that is circular reasoning or "begging the question." The only truth that can be established is the truth that one had the experience. "For to use experience to prove the truth claimed about that experience is to beg the whole question" (Ibid., 77).

Lastly, experiences are capable of different and various interpretations. For example, a naturalist can explain away a miracle, i.e., the resurrection of Jesus, and say that the disciples and those who saw him were simply hallucinating. Another example, is that of a pantheist, who may claim that evil and suffering is a mere illusion and not really real in this world experience. Therefore, the philosophy of experientialism is not plausible and comes up short as a test for what is true and what is false. The difference is that, "Experience is merely a condition of persons; whereas truth is a characteristic of propositions" (Ibid., 81).

Evidentialism

Historic Christianity is a religion that has real and compelling evidence of the life, death, and resurrection of Jesus Christ. Therefore, many Christian apologist appeal to the historical evidences of the past; however, other apologist appeal to evidences of the natural world. There are apologist that appeal to the future or eschatological evidence for verification of the Christian faith. Dodd makes an appeal to the past. Historic Christianity makes its case based upon the fact that there was a series of events that happened as explained by the New Testament gospel writers, i.e., Matthew, Mark, Luke, and John, who claim to be eyewitnesses of this fact.

For Dodd, concerning the historical Jesus, "this triumph is something actually attained not in some coming Day of the Lord, near or distant, but in the concrete historical event of the death and resurrection of Jesus Christ" (Ibid., 87). In terms of Dodd's eschatology, he sees Christianity as a "realized eschatology" that is then realized by the Final Judgement "the relation of all history to the purpose of God. For the essential feature of the Last Judgement is its universality" (Ibid., 87).

Dodd would be considered a historical evidential apologist since he believes that the history of Christianity and its truth is discoverable by examining the historical evidences, such as the death and resurrection of Jesus. Therefore, the resurrection is "the basis and test for truth for one's life and view of the universe. Evidence from the past, and from history, is the basis and test for truth both in the present and the future" (Geisler, 88).

The second appeal to the evidence as a test for truth is that of the example of Paley's analogy of the Watchmaker. William Paley (1743-1805 C.E.) is a proponent well known for the Teleological Argument for God's existence. For he insisted that if someone was walking out in an open field, or a beach by a lake, and found a watch that the person would naturally and rightly conclude that the watch that was found had a watchmaker. Geisler says, "Likewise, if one studies the more complex design found in the natural world, he cannot but conclude that there is a World Designer behind it" (Ibid., 88). This is the basic argument for Paley's teleological argument from present evidence as a test for truth.

The final appeal to evidence as a source of truth is found in John Hick's Eschatological verification. Hick's believed and asserts that there is the fact that everyone will eventually die, and at a person's death, in the future, that person will meet God in the eschaton. Essentially, Hick's believed that, "One's own immortality can be verified if one day he observes his own funeral...God's existence is verifiable in principle if we state the conditions in the next life under which one would recognize that he had met God" (Ibid., 92).

Dodd wishes to demonstrate that the matter of God's

existence is a fact that can be verified upon one's own death. Therefore, truth is verifiable in the eschatological future.

Pragmatism

Pragmatism is the sixth methodology that is survey by Dr. Geisler. To summarize the essence of pragmatism it will be stated that pragmatism is simply defined by way one lives as the meaning of truth. In other words, the pragmatist contends that a human being can't feel the truth, or think the truth; one can simply discover the truth by trying to live the truth. Simply stated, pragmatism is that method of discovering what is true by what "works" best for you. The pragmatic theory is simple: If it works and produces fruit – it must be true! Indeed, Jesus himself said, "by their fruits you shall know them" (Matthew 7:20, NJKV).

A good example of pragmatic theory of truth is that of William James. In his work entitled "Pragmatism" (1907) he wrote that true ideas "are those that we can assimilate, validate, corroborate and unify. False ideas are those that we cannot" (Ibid., 109). James believed truth happens to ideas that we have as people. The ideas are proved to be true as people cash in on their ideas that work in real life application. In banking terms, "Truth lives on a credit system" (Ibid., 109).

Basically, truth is the cash value of an idea put into practice. Pragmatism's test for truth is that it has practical value because it works in real life. So, for James, "If theological ideas should do this, if the notion of God, in particular, should prove to do it, how could pragmatism possibly deny God's existence?" (Ibid., 109).

There has to be pragmatic elements found in Christian apologetics in the history of Christianity itself. For example, as previously mentioned, Jesus himself attributed a practical value in his simple, yet pragmatic statement found in Matthew 7:20 "by their fruits you shall know them." Jesus is the truth, and, as a followers of Jesus we will be those that demonstrate truth in our lives; we believe that Jesus used this metaphor of fruit to illustrate this point.

In terms of contemporary thinkers who were pragmatic in their approach to apologetics, we must consider the insights of the late Francis Schaeffer. In Schaeffer's approach to truth, he believed that man can't live consistent in a non-Christian world view such as that of atheism, or secular humanism. In this respect, man can't live as a simple machine. Crucial to the falsity of a non-Christian view, is that of livability and inconsistency in the life being lived by non-believers. Schaeffer believed that ONLY the Christian can live consistent with their world view of truth.

According to Schaeffer's theory of truth, truth is confirmed by its livability, and experiential application that has real-life verification. "Only the Christian view is consistent and livable, and all non-Christian views are in the final analysis unlivable. Experience confirms this to be true" (Ibid., 111).

The Main weakness of the pragmatic theory of truth is that just because something works, does not necessarily mean it's true. Pragmatism should not be employed by the apologist as a total or complete test for truth. A person can have results in their life, but, this does not mean that they are walking in truth. For example, there are those that live their lives as a thief and steal other people's property, money, etc., and can do quite well for themselves.

So, because someone can live a life as a "thief" does not mean that this is TRUE. As Geisler says, "For many false and evil things have worked for many people for many years. And no finite can see the distant future. Hence pragmatism fails as a sufficient test for truth" (115).

Combinationalism

Philosophers and theologians use a methodology for truth of a world view called "combinationalism" as a "test" for truth. The main reason for this is that the traditional tests for truth, such as, Experientialism , Rationalism, and Evidentialism, etc. are found to be inadequate methods for the testing of a world view in and of itself. In other words, the previous examined methodologies that have been surveyed thus far fall short; therefore, there are some thinkers that use a combination of methods, using more than one single approach to test for the truth. Each combinationalist covered is this chapter "feels that a combination of tests for truth is necessary to establish the truth of a world view" (Ibid., 117).

There are four principles that combinationalist agree on as a test for truth. First, combinational thinkers agree that no ONE test for truth is adequate as a complete test for the truth of a world view. Most agree that there needs to be a least two methods, such as, facticity and rationality are necessary to be employed to establish the truth of a world view, such as Christianity, for example. Second, combinationalists are usually presuppositional in their starting point. In other words, they start with a presupposed set of premises that are not neutral or natural.

Thirdly, the experiences of a person are not self-interpreting. A model or framework is going to be necessary for meaning. Lastly, truth is modeled after a scientific theory or hypothesis. The hypothesis must be tested by its ability to fit the facts; otherwise, it can be falsified. The theory must be tested and found to be consistent in a particular world view.

The main weakness of the combinational method of a test for truth is that one is simply adding ONE inadequate test for truth to another one. It's kind of like adding one leaky bucket to another and another; the first leaky bucket still leaks because the second one does, and so on. The methods surveyed thus far are "leaky buckets" that combined together do not produce a non-leaky bucket methodology. As Geisler states, "by simply adding together inadequate tests for truth one does not get an adequate test for truth" (Ibid., 132).

Adequate Tests for Truth

The methods examined thus far have proven to be either self-defeating, i.e., skepticism and agnosticism, or, have failed as a "stand-alone" test for the truth or falsity of a particular world view. The methods that have been surveyed thus far are ALL found to be wanting and inadequate tests for truth. Geisler, therefore, concludes that there are two tested methods for truth: *UNDENIABILITY* and *UNAFFIRMABILITY* (which is the test for the falsity of a world view).

The purpose of the rest of Geisler's book on *Christian Apologetics* is to "show that all non-theistic world views are directly or indirectly unaffirmable and only theism is affirmable, and, hence, only theism is true" (Ibid., 145). Dr. Geisler further believes that only theism is an affirmable world view that is also *UNDENIALBY TRUE.*

Basically, non-theisms are sayable, that is they can be articulated, but, that does not mean that their meaning is affirmable or justifiable. For example, just because someone believes something and can communicate that belief or world view, it does not prove that the world view or belief is true. Just because someone believes that "Pink

Elephants" on Mars have the answers to life, doesn't make it true, it has to be proven as undeniably true. The proposition by itself can't be proven to have any meaning unless the facts support the proposition.

Moreover, once we establish the fact of a theistic universe in which we live, as the true world view, then, we have to decide "which" one of the theisms, i.e., Judaism, Islam, or Christian Theism, can best fit the facts in the most consistent way, thus theism will be found to be the one and only true theistic view.

Deism

Deism is similar to theism, in that, a deist is one who holds to the view that God is the creator of all that is. However, unlike theism, deism denies the possibility of any type of supernatural involvement with creation. The world was created by God, but, the deist views the world as being self-sustained by natural laws. Basically, deism believes in God, but, the God of creation is a God who is beyond our world and not involved in the sustaining of it. God is, therefore, transcendent but He is NOT immanent.

The "Father" of modern deism is considered to be **Herbert of Cherbury (1583-1648 C.E.).** Thomas Hobbes is considered to be a *materialistic* deist. Other men such as John Locke and Charles Blount, presented a more rationalistic anti-supernatural approach to deism. Deism as a form of Christianity was promoted heavily by the English. For example, **John Toland (1670-1722 C.E.)** believed that miracles as proof of revelation are limited to Moses and Jesus. Toland also rejected anything in Christianity that was mysterious or beyond human reason.

Others such as Anthony Cooper, Anthony Collins, William Wollaston, Thomas Woolston, and Matthew Tindal, all contributed to the propagation of deism in the English world of theology. Also, American deism flourished in the writings of Thomas Jefferson, Benjamin Franklin, and Thomas Paine (who is well known for his book, "The Age of Reason").

Deism is an inadequate world view because miracles

and supernatural intervention of a personal God with His creation is not plausible, according to the view of deism. We reject this view because although it acknowledges God's transcendence, the view fails to give credit to God as being a personal God; He is not just a God who created a Watch and just left it to tick on its own. For these reasons, and many more, deism fails to stand as a proper and truthful world view.

Pantheism

Pantheism is the exact opposite of deism. As surveyed in the previous section on deism, this is the belief that God is other worldly or transcended in nature and being. In pantheism, God is in the world; more specifically, God IS THE WORLD. There are at least four kinds of pantheism that exists: Absolute Pantheism, Emanational Pantheism (the philosopher, Plotinus, held this view), and Developmental Pantheism (this is the view that God unfolds in a historical or evolutionary way); Hegel believed that God unfolds historically. Finally, there is

Manifestational, or Multilevel Pantheisms, that are found in various forms of Hinduism.

The positive aspects of pantheism are as follows: first, pantheism attempts to be comprehensive as a world view. Pantheism is an all embracing world view, God is ALL. Second, pantheism presents God in a personal way whereby He is involved with the world. This world view presents God as being really in the world and is immanent. Thirdly, pantheism does acknowledge that God is absolute and necessary. According to pantheism, no part of creation is independent from GOD. All of creation is completely dependent on Him—who is ALL in ALL.

The negative aspect of pantheism is that there is no such concept as I-Thou relationships between our finite selves and the infinite God. This is because ALL is ONE. There are no metaphysical or intellectual distinctions made in pantheism. In addition to this, when it comes to the problem of evil, pantheism is ship wrecked, because, in the pantheistic world view, evil is simply an illusion. In other words, evil is not real, it doesn't really exist, it's just all in one's mind.

This view presents a very shallow and hollow explanation to those who are suffering the death of a loved one, for example. In pantheism, there simply is no proper distinction between good and evil in this world view. Finally, as a criticism of this view, pantheism presents a view of God that is not personal. In Christianity, God is a loving Father who shows his kindness by providentially caring and interacting with his creation. In pantheism, according to Dr. Geisler, "A personal God—if there is one— is at best a lower manifestation or appearance of the highest impersonal reality" (Ibid., 189).

We conclude on a positive note, that, the pantheist provides insights into the absoluteness of God, the immanence of God in the world, and the unity of being. Pantheism attempts to provide a comprehensive all-embracing philosophy.

Charles Craig Lantz, ThD, PhD

Panentheism

The concept of Panentheism, pronounced "pan-en-theism" is not the same as the world view of pantheism. The latter is the belief that God is the world and therefore, the world is GOD. The former, on the other hand, is the belief that God is in the world much like the way a soul or mind is in the body.

In contemporary theology, this view is known as process theology. This is the theological view that God is always changing and is a finite God that is bi-polar. This is an organic view theologically because of the stress of the fluidity of the world process. What makes God bi-polar in this view is that God has two poles: "a potential pole that is beyond the world and an actual pole which is the physical world" (Ibid., 206). Panentheism is basically a world view that is half-way between traditional theism and pantheism.

As already examined, pantheism is the view that God is ALL REALITY. This entails the Greek mythology that was pervasive in ancient Greek culture with this view;

the Greek gods are present, theologically speaking.

Positively, Panentheism provides some plausible arguments for the existence of God, a rejection of pantheism's view of God and the world. It has also stressed the immanence of God and has rejected a static view of a God that is inactive in the world. It presents a view of God that God is ceaseless in His engagement with our world, and its on-going activity.

Negatively, Panentheism fails as an adequate world view because it presents a view of God as a finite being who changes with the world and reality. A finite God can't guarantee the defeat of evil and the ultimate triumph of good over evil, as theism can. The claim of panentheism is not a biblical view of God; the God of theism is more sufficient in explaining reality both personally and metaphysically.

Atheism

Atheism is the view of reality that there is NO GOD. There is no God in the world or beyond the world. Simply put, atheism contends that there is NO God, or little god, or any kind, or anywhere. Traditionally speaking, this would be the view of philosopher Jean-Paul Sarte, "who believe that there never was, is, or will be a God" (Ibid., 215). Others, like Nietzsche, "believed that the God-myth was once alive, that is, it was a model men believed and lived by, but that this myth died and is no longer workable" (Ibid., 215-216).

Albert Camus argued that theism is contrary to humanitarianism in the follow way: Camus wrote a book called "The Plague" which basically contends that we must either fight the plague of rats that were sent by God on a sinful city, or join the priest (who refuses to fight the plague because that would mean you are fighting against the God who sent the plague).

Camus argued that to fight the plague is to fight against God, which, he argued, would make one anti-humanitarian. Moreover, if theism is right, then, humanitarianism is wrong. So, to be an atheist, that it is, according to Camus, is to be humanitarian because one fights the plague of rats sent to sinful man. We reject this view of Camus as in adequate.

Atheism as a world view that attempts to explain reality fails for the following reasons: (1) The atheist has to assume that matter, plus time, gave rise to MIND. Or, that the impersonal gave rise to the personal. Atheism simply argues against logic because it is more reasonable to believe that MIND formed MATTER, rather than matter forming mind out of nothing, or that matter evolved a MIND; (2) atheism fails to answer the question, "Why is there something rather than nothing?"

In conclusion, atheism holds the absurd position that SOMETHING comes from NOTHING, "that is, that non-being is the ground upon which being rests. This seems highly unreasonable" (Ibid., 234). We believe that God made SOMETHING out of NOTHING, that is ex-nihilo, and therefore, the creation came into existence from an intelligent mind that formed matter, not the other way around. This, then, concludes our summary of atheism as a world view. It takes more faith to be an atheist than it does to be a theist.

Theism

The final world view that will be examined is theism. This view is not a self-defeating view as many of the previous views we have examined are. Theism is the most reasonable view to hold and believe. Basically, it takes more faith to be an atheist than it does to be an honest theist. Dr. Geisler proves the existence of God from the following logical argument: (1) Some things undeniably exists (for example, I can't deny my own existence); (2) my non-existence is possible; (3) whatever has the possibility to not exists is currently caused to exist by another; (4) there can't be an infinite regress of current causes of existence; (5) therefore, a first uncaused cause of my current existence exits; (6) this uncaused cause must be infinite, unchanging, all-powerful, all-knowing, and all-perfect; (7) this infinitely perfect being is called "God"; (8) therefore, God exists; (9)

this God who exists is identical to the God in the Christian Scriptures; (10) therefore, the God described in the Bible exists (Ibid., 238-239).

Theism is the only adequate and sufficient world view to have since it is not self-defeating and actually can be affirmed. The argument presented above by Dr. Geisler leads to the logical explanation, which is more reasonable than any other world view, that there exists an infinitely powerful Being beyond this world that is the final and ONLY UNCAUSED CAUSE OF ALL THAT EXISTS.....GOD is the sustaining first cause and source of all finite, created, changing, and contingent beings. "Theism has found a firm ground in existence for the conclusion that God exists. This is a theistic universe" (Ibid., 258).

Naturalism and Super-naturalism

We have already discussed in the previous section that the world view of theism is true and provable, at least logically reasonable, to believe, which means that God exists. And, if God who created the world exists, then, it follows that He can "ACT" in the world in the realm of the supernatural. Philosophers and skeptics alike have always argued against the possibility of miracles because they believe that the world or nature is run simply by natural laws. Anything that happens out of the ordinary is always explained away by natural causes. For example, Anthony Flew, argues that "everything that happens in the natural world is caused by the natural world" (Ibid., 269).

The possibility of miracles will follow from the nature of a theistic universe created by God. Dr. Geisler lays out the following argument for miracles as follows: (1) An omnipotent, all-knowing, and all-good God exist. (2) Now an all-powerful God can do anything possible. (3) Miracles are not impossibilities. (4) Therefore, it is possible that miracles can occur (Ibid., 279). This concludes our summary that possibility of the supernatural exists and that miracles can take place.

Charles Craig Lantz, ThD, PhD

Objectivism and History

Christianity is a historical religion. The truth of Jesus' life and ministry makes historical claims about miraculous events that confirm these truth claims. The objectiveness of Christianity is that it is based upon real facts of history. The facts that can be verified by the gospel writers, and secular writers, such as Flavius Josephus, a Jewish first century historian, who refers to a man named Jesus, in many of his writings; this confirms the historical value and truthfulness of the religion of Christianity started by the God-man, Jesus Christ.

We have argued, that theism is the correct world view; as such, there is an objective meaning in the world because of real "facts" of historically documented people, places, and historical events. "Hence, objectivity in history is possible, since in a theistic world history would be His-story. Objectivity is possible within a world view" (Ibid., 292).

Charles Craig Lantz, ThD, PhD

The Historical Reliability of the New Testament

In order to establish an apologetic concerning the reliability of the New Testament, three elements will be necessary in establishing this claim. First, the extant manuscripts must be examined. The New Testament documents were written in the Greek language, and we have currently over 5,800 ancient Greek manuscripts that contain portions or sections, or sometimes whole books of the New Testament. These ancient witnesses date very far back into the ancient world, going back as far as the first century in the case of the *John Rylands fragments*, commonly known as P52 which dates somewhere between 117-138 C.E. We also have P66, P72, and P75, which are papyri fragments dated around 200 C.E.

In addition to this, we have full books of the New Testament such as Codex Ephraemi Rescriptus (C), Codex Alexandrinus (A), and Codex Bezae (D). These manuscripts date from the second to the fourth century as witnesses to the events, and the life and teaching of Jesus Christ, and the apostolic beginnings of the early church. According to Dr. Bruce Metzger, we have 76 papyri, 250 uncials, 2,646 minuscules, and 1,997 lectionaries manuscripts. "No other book from antiquity possess anything like this abundance of manuscripts" (Ibid., 306-307). Second, we have an early dating of the New Testament documents that takes us within approximately 30-50 years of the original eyewitness accounts themselves. "This means that the New Testament records are authentic first century and firsthand information about the life, teachings, death, and resurrection of Christ" (Ibid., 313). Third, we have the integrity of the New Testament writers who were eyewitnesses to the events and ministry of Jesus Christ. Also, it is a historical fact that all 12 Apostles died the death of a martyr. This is truly an amazing fact of history, since, if someone knows that something is truly "false" it is hardly reasonable to assume that the person would die for a falsehood.

Most people would not likely give their life for

someone or something that they believe in anyway. The fact that we have the apostolic witness testimony in the first century, and the historical proof that the original 12 apostles died martyr's deaths (see Foxes Book of Martyr's), there can be little doubt as to the reliability and historical truthfulness of the ministry of Jesus. The lives that were changed immediately and the world wide spread of the gospel in the first century, not to mention all the killings of believers, children, and outrageous acts of the Emperors of Rome against this new Christian religion, the apostolic witness and testimony is TRUE. Therefore, the New Testament documents are proven to be reliable witnesses.

The Deity and Authority of Jesus Christ

Historical Christianity in its true orthodox form claims that Jesus Christ was not only a human being, and a real historical figure, but, that he was God in human form. In other words, Jesus was the living God in human flesh. This is the central key-theological truth that distinguishes Christianity from all other world religions and counterfeit forms of Christianity, such as, the Jehovah Witnesses, Mormonism, and Scientology, to name just a few. What makes the Christian religion authoritative and unique is that Jesus was God in human form. He came down from heaven to lift us up out of our life of sin which has separated us from God. Jesus also claimed to be JEHOVAH of the Old Testament (See John 8:58 and 10:31-33).

Jesus claimed to be equal with God several times in the gospel records; he claimed to be the Messiah and accepted divine worship as Lord and God; he had commanding authority to heal the sick and drive out demons. Jesus Christ fulfilled over 300 Old Testament Messianic Prophecies that were made hundreds of years in advance (See Genesis 3:15; cf. Galatians 4:4). Finally, the biggest evidence we have about Jesus is the resurrection that confirms His Deity.

Both Jesus and the Old Testament Prophets predicted the resurrection. For example, we have key Messianic passages in Psalm 2 and 16 that are cited in the

New Testament as being fulfilled in Jesus Christ (**See Acts 2:27ff. and Hebrews 1:5**). Jesus resurrected as the risen Lord and appeared to the apostles several times and appeared to over 500 people who saw him as the risen Christ (See I Cor. 15:5).

The Inspiration and Authority of the Bible

Dr. Geisler states, "Both direct and indirect references unmistakably manifest their affirmation that the Old Testament writings are the inscripturated Word of God" (Ibid., 353). The Apostle Paul wrote that "all Scripture is inspired of God" (II Timothy 3:16). The Greek word for inspired means *God-breathed.* Paul was referring to the entire Old Testament, and to whatever was already considered by the Church to be inspired writings. Jesus also endorsed the entire 39 canonical books of the Old Testament (See John 10:35). The same Holy Spirit that inspired the writers of the Old Testament books is the same Holy Spirit that inspired the 27 New Testament canonical books.

Moreover, the inspiration was not just the thoughts in their minds about what God wanted to say, it is the very WORDS of God. For example, in Exodus 24:4, Moses wrote "all of God's words." The inspiration of the Bible as a whole book is also to be understood in the sense that it is "plenary" which means that whatever the Bible teaches is true. This means that statements made in the Bible are actually true, not false. This would extend to everything the Bible teaches whether spiritual or factual.

The Orthodox Christian view is that there are only 39 canonical Old Testament books, the Law, the Prophets, and the Writings, and 27 New Testament books that are truly the inspired Words of the living God. These books are inspired by the Holy Spirit, written by man, and are authoritative in all matters of Christian faith and practice.

The Roman Catholic church, the false church, or whore of Babylon, recognizes 14 more books called the "apocrypha" or "deuteron-canonical" books as part of the canonical scriptures. This view we reject as not having been recognized by Jesus, or the apostles, therefore, are not inspired of God. Jesus taught that only the 39 books of the Old Testament are the inspired books. We also now have the 27 New Testament books as inspired; this makes for a total of 66 canonical books.

We will close with the following remarks by Dr. Norman Geisler: "with these sixty-six books we have the complete and final revelation of God for faith and practice of believers. Every spirit or prophet who claims to give a new or different revelation is not of God" (Ibid., 376).

Charles Craig Lantz, ThD, PhD

CHAPTER TWO

APOLOGETICS II: REASONABLE FAITH[1]

Faith and Reason: How Do I know Christianity Is true?

The title of Chapter One "Faith and Reason" is the subject of an age old issue that goes back many centuries, back into the great thinkers of Church history. Great thinkers such as **St. Augustine (354-430 C.E.)** spent much time reflecting about the *relationship between faith and reason*. It was enough for Augustine to accept the truth of Jesus Christ simply on the basis of the authority of the Scriptures.

For Augustine, the Scriptures have authority on the basis of fulfilled prophecy and miracles, such as the

---

1   The primary source of information for this essay is from the book, *Reasonable Faith: Christian Truth and Apologetics*, by Dr. William Lane Craig, who is considered by the Evangelical World the Premier Christian Apologist. He has authored several books on the subject of Apologetics, and is best known for his work on the *Kalam Cosmological Argument for the Existence of God*, which was his doctoral thesis for the ThD degree. See *Reasonable Faith* by Dr. Craig, published by Moody Press, Chicago, Ill: Revised Edition, 1994.

resurrection, and the miracles that were performed by Christ that are recorded in the reliable testimony of the gospel writers, such as, Matthew, Mark, Luke, and John. In addition to this evidence, we have authentic **eye-witnesses**. We therefore have the unique testimony of the living Church as a community entity that testifies of the truth and authority of the Scriptures as the primary ground and reason for faith.

Dr. Craig does an excellent job at surveying the following thinkers and explaining their understanding of the unique relationship between faith and reason in the following men: Thomas Aquinas - who was primarily a natural theologian, meaning that faith was essentially intellectual assent to doctrines not provable by reason-hence, Aquinas believed that doctrine can not be both known (reason) and believed by faith (See Craig, 1994, 22). The Enlightenment period, known as *The Age of Reason*, was highly influenced by John Locke and Henry Dodwell.

These men were considered theological rationalist. In

other words, they sought to give philosophical explanations to the issues of faith. Locke argued for the existence of God by rational explanations such as the "Cosmological Argument" for the existence of God. At the other end of the rationalistic approach during this period, Dodwell makes an anti-rational religious tradition that taught that the way to God is not the intellect, but, the means of the heart. Faith is simply a gift that the person elected by God has been given by the means of the Holy Spirit.

On the contemporary scene, Karl Barth and Rudolph Bultmann were the predominant thinkers during the early 19th century, which by then, German critical scholarship had taken deep roots in the Universities of Europe. By this time, scholars were no longer taking seriously the historical accounts of the gospel; they were not seen or believed to be actual events that happened, much as legends that circulated in the early Church and were finally written down. Most of the supernatural aspects of the ministry of Jesus found in the gospel records are dismissed as "myths" by Bultmann and his followers.

Dr. Craig goes on in chapter one explaining how we can know Christianity to be true. He first mentions the role of the Holy Spirit as a self-authenticating witness. Craig then surveys the Scriptural teaching on the role of the Holy Spirit in the born-again experience, being added to the body of Christ, water baptism and the work of sanctification, which is all the work of the indwelling of God's spirit in our lives.

The Holy Spirit is the primary agent that is responsible for convicting the hearts of men, women, and young people, of their sins and that they are in need of a savior. Without the ministry of the spirit's work in our lives, we would be left destitute in our sins and separated from a loving God.

In the later part of chapter one, Dr. Craig begins to explain the role of systematic reason and logic in the role of evangelism. The clear facts of the matter are that no one can come to Christ unless the Father draws them to Himself;

Jesus taught this in John Chapter 15. However, in the process of being drawn it is not uncommon for questions and road blocks that begin to crop up in the minds of non-believers, most of the time. This is especially true on college and university campus settings. People who come to Christ have questions that need to be answered by intelligent Christians, and this is the whole point and purpose of Craig's book that we are currently taking a survey of. Craig makes it clear that apologetics can not produce 100 percent certainty, it can only be used by Christians to produce probability.

Apologetics and the practical application of it is ultimately designed to be useful in conversations with unsaved people. Most of these types of arguments that are used to convince someone that God exists will most likely be used in a College or University setting. As an adult worker in the "real" world, I find that people usually have already made up their minds one way or another. I worked with college and university students in campus ministry at

MSU for over 17 years, and most of the time these apologetic applications were used either in one-to-one evangelism, open-air preaching, or some type of outreach to students in a multi-media format.

The purpose of apologetics is to equip us as believers to be ready to defend the faith according to I Peter 3:15, which states, "but sanctify Christ as Lord in your hearts, always being ready to make a defense to everyone who asks you to give an account of the hope that is in you...." (The Apostle Peter). This is the call of all Christians and therefore, the subject of apologetics must be taken seriously by the body of Christ at large.

The Absurdity of Life Without God

If then there is NO GOD, then life on this planet really is just pointless living. If there is no God at all, then, there is no ultimate hope for the universe or mankind, we are at the mercy of nature and whatever happens. Furthermore, we are left with no real clear right and wrong concepts that can govern us as individuals or society. Life without God means that life is absurd and without ultimate significance, value, or purpose.

Life has no ultimate meaning without immortality and God. We have no more purpose and meaning than pigs and mosquitoes, for that matter. Everything that exists now will eventually just come to nothing. This means that because our lives are meaningless, the activities that we do, our jobs, our university and college education has no ultimate value, only the value that we can temporarily place upon it. "This is the horror of modern man: because he ends in nothing, he is nothing" (Craig 1994, 59).

Life without God means no ultimate value as well. In other words, what does it matter if you choose to live your life as Stalin or Mother Teresa? It's all the same, there are no moral values so one can just live totally for self; no one holds you accountable, ultimately. In a world without moral values of right and wrong, who is to judge my actions as good or evil? it's all morally relative. Moral values are just a result of a personal taste or preference; or as a result of socio-biological evolution and social conditioning. So, the concept of morality loses all meaning in a universe without God.

Finally, in a world without God, life has no ultimate purpose. The universe has no purpose and life for the human race means that there is no ultimate purpose. If there is no God then our life is not any different from that of a cat or a dog; just live, eat, drink, and be as merry as you can for the moment, for tomorrow we die. This is the philosophy of the those who embrace atheism. In terms of the universe, again, life without God means that the universe was just a cosmic accident, a random chance of explosion.

As for man, he or she is just a freak of nature, an accident, blind chance of matter plus slime and time that evolved into a rational being somehow. Since the end of everything is death, life is utterly without reason, hope, purpose, and moral value...it just simply is, and that's it. In philosophical terms, this means that the end of God is

NIHILISM.

On the other hand, if there is a God, then mankind and the universe has hope. It means that there is a purpose to our existence, and the universe for that matter. Because atheism leads to nihilism, the other alternative to living is the Christian one. The Christian worldview offers one hope; man's life does not simply end at the grave, there is life after death. So this life is not all that there is and to do, there is life after death, and that means that what we do in this life must count for something.

"Atheism has left the world bankrupt and devoid of purpose, value, and hope."

(Dr. William L Craig)

By comparing these two worldviews, when I was in campus ministry at Michigan State University (1987-2004), I had the privilege of sharing the gospel with some pretty sharp intellectual kids, yet most of them lived a life of self indulgence. It was my job to set up Bible studies in the dorms, promote outreaches and bring in evangelists from other places. We used multi-media presentations in different formats addressing different issues and topics.

The atheistic world view is on the rise in college and university settings. Most students who adopt these philosophies and outlooks, usually develop an ethic that is relative to their needs, wants, and desires.

When speaking individually with students, I would ask them if they considered it morally wrong to rape little babies and murder people. When cutting to the core like this, you go right for the jugular vein because everyone knows that these actions are not right in man's eyes or society. By using this illustration (which is extreme), I did get through to them in most cases and I was able to show them that even the most base of people know that this is not right. So then it "begs the question", where did this sense of right and wrong to not rape babies or murder people come from? Why is it that people almost universally understand this to be wrong? So I have an avenue to now point them back to their Creator/God who is the author of all morality, purpose, and value in life.

The Existence of God

In his book, *Reasonable Faith*, Dr. Craig lectures on the arguments for God's existence on a rational level. He does make it clear that the arguments themselves can't PROVE the existence of God. The reality is that you can not prove the existence of God, but you can't disprove it either. The arguments that are laid out in this lecture/chapter are designed to get the unbeliever to think about the possibility that God does exist using logic and reason. Through logic and reason, this will aid the one sharing the Gospel, in whatever format, to give compelling critical thinking and evidence that God does in fact exist.

There are a couple of passages of Scripture that are noteworthy and relevant to the discussion at hand. First, Psalms 19:1 says, "The heavens are telling of the glory of God; and their expanse is declaring the work of his hands."

This means that nature itself is telling us that God exists. The beauty of nature and the earth, mountains, rivers, and trees, etc, are telling a story of their creator. In addition to this bit of information, we have the Apostle Paul arguing that "Since the creation of the world His invisible attributes, His eternal power and divine nature, have been clearly seen, being understood through what has been made, so that they (men) are without excuse" (Romans 1:20).

This means that God will not use philosophical arguments on judgment day to prove to us that He exists. He has revealed Himself and mankind already knows this, they just suppress the knowledge of God because of their hard hearts. Most atheists know in their hearts and conscience that God does exist, they just choose to believe that He does not.

Someone once told me, "The mind justifies what the heart desires" meaning that people often times develop their moral philosophy of living because they are seeking to justify a certain type of lifestyle, that, if God does exist, they instinctively know that He would not be OK with them like they are. In other words, they would have to change they way they think, believe, and behave; natural sinful man/women does not want to do such a thing. Having said all of that, let me now summarize these arguments for the existence of God.

The Ontological Argument: This argument attempts to prove that the very concept of "GOD" proves that He does exist. It goes like this, "If God is conceivable, then he must actually exist." **St. Anselm (1033-1109 C.E.)** is the main proponent of the argument, and he reasoned that God is the greatest conceivable of all beings; for if something can be greater that can be conceived, than that conception would be God. Nothing greater than God can be conceived, therefore, God must exist. Everyone knows that God is the greatest conceivable being, so God must exist not merely in the mind, but in reality as well. *Because God is the greatest conceivable being, His non-existence must be inconceivable, therefore, God must exist.*

Charles Craig Lantz, ThD, PhD

The Cosmological Argument: The cosmological argument for God's existence starts with the premise that something, namely the universe exists. So we know that everything that exist, i.e., the universe, this planet, and everything that lives and moves on it, has a cause for its existence. Giraffes don't just pop into existence out of thin air, for example. In terms of the universe, it is now scientifically proven that there was a big bang, so the universe had a beginning, a first cause. This argument seeks to demonstrate that this first cause was God the Creator. Basically, something can not come from nothing. Anything that exists came from something. So, because of this, there must be a FIRST CAUSE of the existence of everything else, which is uncaused: and this is what everyone calls "God." As Dr. Craig puts it, "...the reason for the universe's existence must be found outside the universe, in a being whose sufficient reason is self-contained; it is its own reason for existing and is the reason the universe exists as well. This sufficient reason of all things is God, whose own existence it to be explained only by reference to himself. **That is to say, God is a metaphysically necessary being**" (Ibid., 83).

The Teleological Argument: This argument is the oldest and probably the most popular to use argument since it is simpler and less philosophical. It is commonly known as the "design" argument, or argument from design. Just as we infer that a watch has a designer, a watchmaker, for example, so the universe had a designer too. For that matter, any product that IS we can discern a purposeful adaptation of means to some end (telos). Hence, the name of the argument, Teleological. Thomas Aquinas and William Paley were advocates of the argument from design in the classical sense.

The Moral Argument: This argument for the existence of God came from the logical deduction that God is the embodiment and source of all goodness which is the source of all moral values we can experience in this world. As mentioned before, people have an innate sense of what is basically right and wrong. Because of this moral consciousness in man, it points to a benevolent creator that is the supreme essence of this goodness. **"The moral order is the order of an infinite, eternal Mind who is the architect of nature and whose moral purpose man and the universe are slowly fulfilling"** (Ibid., 90).

Conclusion

This section seeks to demonstrate that there are rational reasons as to why Christians think, or theists for that matter, that God exists. These arguments can be employed through the use of apologetics, and used during evangelistic conversations or lectures, but can not be used demonstratively to prove God's existence. As mentioned in the introduction of this chapter summary, the Scriptures have shown that God has clearly revealed Himself through nature and His awesome creation so that men/women are without excuse to stand before the living God.

The arguments are only tools to be used with unbelievers in terms of convincing them intellectually that there are rational reasons to believe that God exist; this is only the starting point though. *It is the job of the Holy Spirit to convict their hearts, and drawn them into a relationship with the Creator.*

In conclusion, we would have to say that the ontological argument is the least effective. We have found through personal experience that the **teleological argument** has proven to be effective since it is more basic and less abstract and philosophical than the others. In sharing the gospel with someone, you can say something like, "Suppose you were walking along the beach and came across a watch that was ticking that someone had left in the sand, would you dare think that the watch just popped into self-existence without a designer?" Then, allow that person to think about that question and respond to it. This is how that argument can be applied in a real-life application.

The Problem of Miracles

For many people today, and for the past 150 years, people have struggled with Christianity intellectually for the main reason that it is a RELIGION OF MIRACLES, meaning, that the Christian faith is based on the miraculous event of first, the incarnation of Jesus Christ, who is GOD in the flesh, and then, second, that Jesus was crucified, buried for dead, and then resurrected back to life (not in the same exact physical body that He once had, but, a glorified body).

The problem is that these sort of miracles occurred during mans pre-scientific era. The supernaturalist worldview of the pre-scientific era is a superstitious belief system that dominated during the early periods and continued up through the middle ages. After the middle ages, this worldview began to lean more and more towards rationalistic thinking.

By the time of the early 19th century, German radical scholarship was flat out embarrassed to have to acknowledge that type of supernaturalism. A scholar by the name of Rudolf Bultmann, and his followers, simply explained away the supernatural elements of the gospels as mere MYTHS so that there would be no intellectual acknowledgment of the miraculous, and therefore, we can still believe in a man named Jesus, and embrace the ethical kingdom teachings, without committing intellectual suicide, so to speak.

As Craig notes, "According to Bultmann, no one who uses the radio or electric lights should be expected to believe in the mythological world view of the Bible in order to become a Christian" (Ibid., 127). What Bultmann was trying to do was to remove the stumbling block of the supernatural to modern man, so that the essence of the truth of Christianity might be embraced, but, in doing so, Bultmann reduced Christianity to a little more than a religious existential philosophy of a higher goodness. This, however, is not true Christianity.

How do we explain miracles? If we can establish the credible argument that God does exist and that the Big Bang was in reality, the beginning, then, we know that God is the Creator of all Laws of Nature, Physics, and Natural

Laws that govern this world. As Christians, we do acknowledge the fact that God can choose to suspend these Laws if He wants to, as He has many times as illustrated in both Old and New Testaments. Then the fact that He choose to give life to a dead corpse, to a person named Jesus is not only possible, but in all probability based on the evidences that we have, Christians can be certain that Jesus rose from the dead. The Apostle Paul argues that unless the resurrection happened, our faith is null and void.

So, why would the disciples who were scared after Jesus died, suddenly develop an unwavering faith and boldness and endure much persecution, beatings, jail, and martyrdom? The reason is that the disciples, all 12 of them, Jesus physically appeared to them in person after His resurrection. We have excellent eye witness reports of Matthew, Mark, Luke, and John (especially) that give first hand accounts of the things that they had both seen and heard (Luke 1, the prologue).

Also, Paul says that Jesus appeared to over 500 people and that in Acts 9, we have the account of Saul the persecutor of the new Christian faith, being confronted by Jesus on the road to Damascus- which he became one of the greatest followers of Christ and wrote ⅔ of the New Testament, and died as a Martyr under Roman rule and condemnation. These facts alone serve as clear evidence that the resurrection actually happened.

Finally, we want to point out that the first ones that Jesus appeared to were women!!!! Why is this significant? Because women during this time period did not have many rights, and their testimony could not be used in a court of law- so, if the resurrection of Jesus was not true and was a hoax, or a prank, or anything else except a real event, MEN would be the ones recorded as seeing JESUS first, not women.

The fact that the gospel writers all record women as being key early eye-witnesses of the resurrection is a dead giveaway that it was a fact and did happen, otherwise, they would be too embarrassed to record women who had NO RIGHTS in that era as being the ones who Jesus first appeared to, I think this reason alone is most compelling.

This concludes our summary of why I think miracles do happen regardless of what skeptics and critical scholars in history have argued against. Faith in Jesus is real and life changing, it is not just an intellectual ascent to abstract truths that saves someone, it is real heartfelt faith, conviction, and confession, that Jesus is Lord and Savior, Amen!!!!!

The Problem of Historical Knowledge

What makes Christianity so unique is that it is rooted not in philosophy or abstract methods of thought or self inquiry, rather, it is rooted in real events of history. Most other world religions have no way to verify their data; as such, the history of Christianity makes the truth claims of the Jesus Christ difficult for the skeptic to overcome. On the scholarly level, however, the problem is that many scholars of history are relativistic in their thinking. Historical relativism as such, denies the objectivity of historical documentable facts. Historical skepticism then has a profound and often negative impact on such disciplines as apologetics, hermeneutics, and the doctrine of revelation, argues Craig (Ibid., 157). Before we can examine the evidence of the biblical documents themselves, and the impact on what they tell us, it is necessary to examine the "Problem of Historical Knowledge."

Dr. Craig argues that it is during the nineteenth century that we see the greatest advances in the science of history, and the earmark of this period is *objectivity* (Ibid., 166). Basically, the task of the historian is to uncover facts that can be verified, and let those facts speak for themselves. With this quest for objectivity came the quest for the historical Jesus. During this period one scholar after another wrote and tried to explain the historical Jesus in a non-miraculous way. These scholars were trying to rediscover a non-supernatural Jesus. However, eventually the movement ground to a halt because they argued that these miracles did not historically happen and no non-supernatural Jesus could be uncovered in the gospels.

So, rather "than accept the supernatural Jesus as historical, however, biblical critics ascribed that belief to the theology of the early church, which they said so overlaid the traditions about the historical Jesus that he was no longer recoverable" (Craig 1994, 168). Eventually, both dialectical and existential theology divided between what was historical, and what were the theological truths of the gospels without embracing the historical supernatural Jesus. Theologians then, drew a distinction between the historical Jesus and the theology of Jesus. It boiled down to the difference between the Jesus of history and the Christ of faith, so to speak.

The position that a historical relativist takes really is self-refuting. To argue that we can not know certain events that happened in our history simply because we were not there and therefore can not reconstruct them borders on the absurd in thinking. One scholar, for example, Becker, argues that facts exist only in the mind. This scholar argues that facts exists as only statements about the events. In other words, the historian makes statements about events that have happened, but, this does not mean that they actually happened. But this is a ridiculous claim and it is self-refuting for this reason: a historical fact is either the historical events itself or a piece of accurate information about the event or events. Becker's statements that facts exists only in the mind are silly because that would mean that someone like Abraham Lincoln didn't really exist if people forget about him. However, it was Lincoln's absence from history not his presence that made such a difference in U.S. history argues Craig (Ibid., 181).

The reality is that history gets recorded by eyewitnesses, also there is left behind physical evidences that such people, places, things, and events, that actually existed in history and happened too. Therefore, the historian and the scientist have much in common: they arrive at conclusions based on an evaluation of the evidences. Historians can scientifically study such things as archaeology which is the examination of coins, pottery weapons, and other artifacts as evidences to support the hypothesis of certain facts. In other words, what happened in the past is what the evidences indicates as really having happened. History is not just something made up or reconstructed in someone's mind, it is not relativistic, it is probable and in many cases, provable. In essence, the goal of historical knowledge is to obtain probability...not mathematical certainty.

A good example to illustrate this truth is that of a court of law. In a court of law, for example, the verdict is awarded to the one whose case is most probable by the evidence presented to the jury. This jury then is asked to determine if the person being convicted of a certain crime is guilty, and on the basis of *reasonable doubt*. The jury is not asked to make a decision upon whether or not they think he or she is guilty beyond *all doubt*, rather, they are asked to make a decision based upon the evidence presented to them, *beyond all reasonable doubt*, and there is a huge difference between the two concepts. Craig adds, **"It is**

exactly the same in history: we should accept the hypothesis that provides the most probable explanation of the evidence" (184).

The implications for the use of Christian Apologetics is very powerful. We don't have to prove to skeptics with 100 percent certainty that Christianity is true or that God exist, for example. We are only required to provide and point to reasonable explanations of our faith whether that be personal testimony of a changed life, an argument for the existence of God, or the pointing to the historical documents of history that explain that there was a person named Jesus who existed from many historical sources, and people have to deal with this simple fact. Whether or not we convince someone of these truths is not our ultimate responsibility, that is the job of the Holy Spirit of God.

By presenting simple arguments and evidence for the Christian faith, we can be confident that we have enough evidence to show that Jesus lived, died, and resurrected, beyond a reasonable doubt, not beyond all doubt, but, the Jesus of history can be explained beyond all reasonable doubt. And that's good enough. This concludes our summary of *The Problem of Historical Knowledge.*

The Historical Reliability of the New Testament

The central core issue of this section deals with the trustworthiness of the New Testament documents themselves. We will examine some of the historical evidence that support the overall reliability of the New Testament (from here on will be abbreviated as NT). "There are also a good many critics around the globe that have doubted the authenticity and accuracy of these documents after they were written down long ago" (Blomberg quoted in Craig 1994, 193). However, to combat this doubt, scholars around the world have developed a scientific method known as **Textual Criticism** which essentially is used to uncover the original readings from the thousands of NT manuscripts. Moreover, this science of comparing ancient manuscripts (from here on will be abbreviated as MS or MSS plural) and classifying them into families and categories, has left the doubts of liberal scholars without any foundation whatsoever.

Just as an illustration of this evidence, without going into excessive details, the oldest MS evidence that we have is on a scrap of papyrus, known as P52, that contains a small portion of John's Gospel (See John 18:31-33; 37-38) which dates from no earlier than 125-130 C.E. Scholars believe that this would make the dating of the gospel only about 40 years after the oral traditions were written down, about 90 C.E. There are now more than 130 papyri fragments some of them date no later than the third century. For example, P45 contains most of the gospels and the book of Acts; we also have the letters of Paul found in P46, and, we have four very early dated almost complete NTs found in Codex Aleph, Beta, Alexandrian, and C.

There are currently more than 5,800 MSS in Greek that contain portions and fragments of the NT. In all of this, there is an overwhelming evidence of the attestation to the veracity of the gospel writings with complete authenticity of the whole and complete 27 NT Canonical books. There is no doubt in most conservative scholars minds, that the books that we have called the NT are the Words of God that written down now almost 2000 years ago.

Scholars have concluded that there are only about 400 major variants or variations between the MS evidence, and most of the variants are minor and have to do with spelling, punctuation, and duplication of words or phrases (Ibid., 194). None of the textual variants have any effect on the content and meaning of major Bible doctrines that have any significance. There are two passages of scripture that scholars have debated about whether or not they were originally in the historical documents; these passages are the women caught in adultery (John 7:53- 8:11) and the longer ending found in Mark's gospel (Mark 16:9-20).

Most scholars don't deny that the story of the women caught in adultery is authentic, but, they question whether or not John actually wrote the story in the original documents themselves. These two passages are hotly contested on both sides, but, the fact is that based on raw historical data, these passages are not found in the earliest surviving Codices that we have, which are Codex Aleph and B. At any rate, 99% of the NT can be completely reconstructed based on these documents "beyond any reasonable doubt, and no Christian doctrine is founded solely or even primarily on textually disputed passages" (Blomberg quoted in Craig 1994, 194). This is the BIG PICTURE.

Blomberg wrote this particular chapter in Craig's book that we are surveying, and he makes a valid point that the burden of proof to disprove the authenticity of the NT is a burden that must be on the shoulder's of the skeptics. It is true that there are some apparent discrepancies in the gospels that on the surface appear to be contradictions. However, upon further examination of these particular texts, we can see that the gospel writers all wrote from their particular viewpoint and theological perspective. Therefore, they are not contradictory but rather are supplementary in nature as they each supply their own details of the ministry of Jesus, and His crucifixion and consequent resurrection.

In summary, the texts of the surviving MSS of the NT far outweigh the number of surviving MSS of other ancient documents of antiquity. Most of the writers of the NT were eyewitnesses as well, they simply wrote down what they have both seen and heard, as John records in his prologue in John chapter one. Matthew was a direct eyewitness and Mark's gospel contains essentially the oral traditions and teachings of the Apostle Peter. In addition to this, we have Luke who was a physician who carefully recorded the data of what he had seen and heard from Paul and other eyewitnesses around the hub of all the religious activity which is in Jerusalem.

These evangelist did record (with great accuracy) the teachings and truths of Jesus Christ, and laid an apostolic foundation for the Church that emerged and thrived in the centuries to come, precisely because of their testimony to the life and ministry of the Lord Jesus Christ. As Blomberg says, "Belief in the veracity of the words and claims of Jesus and the apostles is the next logical step but takes us beyond the bounds of an investigation of the historical reliability of the documents" (Ibid., 227). This concludes our summary of chapter six in brief.

The Self-Understanding of Jesus

This chapter deals with the issue of how Jesus understood himself. Did he think that he was a great teacher on ethics and the kingdom of God? Did he think that he was a miracle worker? Did he think of himself as the Messiah that came to save Israel from the dominance of Rome? There is no question, argues Craig, that the Christian Religion stands or falls depending on WHO Jesus was. The fact is, that when we compare the teachings of Christ and the history of the resurrection account, Jesus stands out as a unique person in history.

Moreover, Judaism continues without such people as Moses; Islam continues without Mohamed, but,

Christianity could not survive without Christ.....If Christ is still in the tomb and buried, the Christian faith crumbles at the very foundation.

This chapter is an attempt on Craig's part to survey some of the historical movements and views of scholars as to who was the real historical Jesus. The most recent attempt to recover who Jesus was is the Life of Jesus movement. This is where European scholars and theological thought come into the discussion at hand. As Craig emphatically states: "The chief effort of this quest was to write a life of Jesus as it supposedly really was, without the supernatural accretions found in the gospels" (Ibid., 233).

The life of Jesus movement did not recover a Jesus who was supernatural. At whatever conclusions the scholars came to in the life of Jesus, it was not a supernatural deity that actually did miracles and touch lives in a supernatural way, so they claim. Much of the supernatural that is found in the gospels are explained away as "Myths" about Jesus that the early church simply wrote back into the gospel records, hence, no such events actually can be proved to have happened. Such is the view of the Higher Critical Schools of theology in Europe and Germany, in particular.

An example of this type of thinking is found in a scholar by the name of Albert Schweitzer who believed and wrote that we do not know who Jesus really was, and, that he was just a man unknown. What we do know claimed Schweitzer, was that Jesus was not a supernatural man at all, but, that Jesus only believed that he was an eschatological figure who claimed to usher in the Kingdom of God. As a skeptic, then, Schweitzer was influential in bringing back to focus the eschatological nature of the Kingdom of God in the teaching ministry of Jesus. This movement did not believe that an accurate biography of Jesus was written down by the claimed author's, rather, it was only possible to extract the Christ of faith and not the Jesus of history. The Jesus of history has been colored by the early Christian theology of the early Church, such historical events probably never happened at all.

In addition to this, there also emerged in Germany a scholar by the name of Karl Barth, who was a dialectical and existential theologian. Barth believed that it is not the Jesus of history in the gospel records that impacts us today, he believed that it is the Christ of faith that is proclaimed by the church that encounters us today (Ibid., 236). Another German scholar, Rudolf Bultmann, as mentioned already in this book, believed that, all that Jesus actually spoke and did could be recorded on a 4" x 6" index card, in other words, this little bit of space contained the historical verifiable words and works of Jesus that Bultmann believed were actually true!!!!! But to these two theologians the truth of historical events of Jesus were subsequently inconsequential because it is the Christ that is proclaimed by the Church today that one encounters. So, for them, the historical and factual data is not really relevant anyways.

According to Craig, as we come to the end of the

twentieth century after the death of Jesus, it must be pointed out that men and women continue to be concerned and perplexed as to the identity of Jesus, he will continue to be a fascination in the minds of the curious. Although the critical scholars and contemporary skeptics continue to deny his power and authority in their lives by their fig leaf of unbelief, Christ's divinity and His soteriological work can be defended as follows:

(1) *Jesus thought of himself as being the Son of God in a unique way.* Jesus called God "abba" meaning Papa or daddy, it needs to be stated that no Jew would dare call God his "daddy" that was way to personal. But Jesus came to reveal the personal nature of the father. In the gospels (See Mark 12:1-9) Jesus tells a parable that reveals the self-understanding of Jesus as God's special Son. Jesus reveals himself in the gospels as the special messenger, and a final one, that was the rightful heir to be the King of Israel. Jesus claimed to be the absolute revelation of God in the flesh- to

see him was to see the father, for he was an exact representation of his glory and divine nature.

(2) *Jesus claimed to act and speak with divine authority.* Jesus was called Rabbi and he sought to claim a higher authority than that of the scribes and pharisees on the basis that Christ changed the interpretations of the Law of Moses in the Sermon on the Mount, and he forgave sins as well. No Jew who was a religious leader in Judaism would dare to pronounce forgiveness of sins or adjust the interpretations of the Laws of Moses- by doing so Jesus was exerting his authority as GOD. Also, the fact that Jesus confronted demons and cast them out as an exorcist was also a demonstration that he had unique authority and power. These supernatural aspects of the ministry of Jesus point out a couple of truths, one, they show that Jesus claimed divine authority over the forces of darkness, and two, Jesus believed that in himself the Kingdom of God had come and manifested itself on earth through God's power. By demonstrating his kingdom power and authority, he

was subtly declaring himself to be GOD.

(3) *Jesus believed himself able to perform miracles.* These miracles were taken to be signs of the in-breaking of the Kingdom of God into Jewish life and thought. Also, Jesus was able to perform healing and miracles over all forms of diseases and infirmities- this also is a claim to his divinity.

(4) *Jesus claimed to determine people's eternal destiny before God.* In Jesus' ministry, he makes it clear that depending on how you received him would determine your ultimate destiny - either in paradise or eternal hell fire. For example, in Luke 12:8-9, Jesus basically says if you deny the Son of man before men, he will deny you before the angels and his father, which essentially means you would be cast out of heaven and spend an eternity separated from him in agony and flames. This is the clear teaching of the entire NT, and OT, for that matter. In other words, Jesus claimed that their eternal destinies were on the line on the basis of how they responded to him...wow, that is so powerful. As Craig notes, "For Jesus is saying that people's salvation depends

on their confession to Jesus himself" (Ibid., 251).

The Resurrection of Jesus

I will do my best to summarize and highlight the main points and arguments that Craig makes in regards to the historical evidence for the resurrection of Jesus, and the skeptics arguments against the fact of its historicity. Essentially, the logical boils down to this: "If Jesus rose from the dead, then his claims are vindicated and our Christian hope is sure; if Jesus did not rise, our faith is futile and we fall back into despair" argues Craig (Ibid., 255).

Moreover, I would like to argue and say that the fact of the resurrection is either true or it is not; it's as simple as that. If we can demonstrate in this summary that there is a reasonable amount of evidence to convince the skeptic that the resurrection is most probably true, then it is an endeavor worthy of investigation.

We will present Craig's arguments for the traditional evidence for historical apologetics, which are based upon some the arguments in defense of the apostolic authorship of the gospels and NT documents. If one can argue from a classical historical apologetical perspective, all one has to do is demonstrate that the authors of the gospels were authentic, and then one is presented with the fact of the resurrection and therefore one must make a choice to accept or reject the premise of the resurrection. Without going into excessive details, Craig argues that we have both internal and external evidence that the authors of the documents were eyewitnesses and therefore reliable testimonies of the historical account given in the narratives themselves.

Internally, the gospels "are full of proper names, dates, cultural details, historical events, and customs and opinions of that time" (Ibid., 256). In terms of external evidences, we have numerous writings and testimonies of the Apostolic Church Fathers, and other Theologians in the second and third century, that would attribute such writings to apostolic authenticity/authority, such as, *Theophilus, Hippolitus, Origen, Irenaeus, Melito, Polycarp,*

Justin Martyr, Dionysius, Tertullian, and Cyprian, were all aware of the Scriptures and considered them as having Divine Inspiration in their writings and quotations, and also testified unanimously that Jesus had resurrected from the dead (Ibid., 256-257).

Having demonstrated that the gospels are reliable and authentic, we are now in a position to argue that the gospels are HISTORICALLY reliable accounts of the life and ministry of Jesus, and all attest to his death, burial, and resurrection. If however, these accounts are false, then, the apostles were either deceived or were deceivers. One of the biggest facts that the gospel attest to is that it was WOMEN that Jesus appeared to first. This alone would convince me that the accounts are true since, back in that day, women were second-class citizens, and were not worthy of being a witness in a court of Law, men however were, and if the disciples were fabricating lies to convince the Jewish leaders, and the general public to get followers, they most assuredly would have recorded that men were the first ones to see the risen Christ.

The fact that the gospels even record that data that Jesus appeared to women first, is a dead giveaway that they were not lying about the facts, and simply recording the story as it actually happened. In addition to this, it would have been impossible for the disciples to believe and preach like they did if their Master was still dead in the grave. The disciples were bold in their faith and declarations of the risen Lord, and certainly would not have been beaten, imprisoned, and died martyrs death if all of this was one big lie. Also, this new religion called "Christianity" emerged right from Jerusalem, the heart of where the Lord was crucified.

It is unlikely that they could overcome such opposition to their message and faith for all the Jewish leaders would have to do is show someone the tomb with a dead corpse in it, but, there was no dead body around anywhere to be found. All the Jewish leaders could do is fabricate the lie that the disciples stole the body. Craig points out that around 64 C.E. Nero, the Emperor of Rome, heavily persecuted the Christians. For example, about 34 years after Jesus' death, the Christian religion was such a threat to Imperial Roman Power that Nero had Christians clothed in wild animal skins and had them devoured by hungry lions while others were smeared with pitch and lighted with fire to become martyrs as **human torches** while events were going on in the evening (Ibid., 262).

We have the writings of such people as Pliny the Younger, Martial, Epictetus, and Marcus Aurelius, that believers were being tourchured to death rather than renouncing their faith in the Jesus who is the resurrected Lord and King!!!! This is so powerful of a testimony that it is hard to imagine that the apostles were deceived or were deceivers of the new found faith. Why? **because in hundreds if not thousands of cases, it lead to death by torture.** That is why we as Christians can make such a strong argument that the historical documents are true and the fact that Christianity started under such horrible circumstances continued to grow without being stamped out which was the intention of such persecutors. In light of this, *Why not believe the testimony of these gospel writers?*

During the late 1700s and 1800s the decline of historical apologetics began to happen through the writings of such men as Herrmann Samuel Reimarus, professor at Hamburg University. According to Craig (Ibid., 266) Reimarus privately had gnawing doubts about the truth found in biblical writings concerning the resurrection, etc. In secret, he wrote a 4,000 page critical evaluation of the bible calling into question the historical events like the Flood, and the story of Moses and Pharaoh, and of course, this led to his doubts about the resurrection of Jesus.

These secret writings were published posthumously by a Librarian by the name of Gottfried Lessing, which attacked the historicity of Jesus' resurrection which lead to a major uproar in terms of German Orthodoxy. These and other attacks like this eventually led to the demise of historical apologetics in the classical sense. By the early

1900's the tide of subjectivism was in full force against traditional theology. So, traditional apologetics moved away from objective evidences to subjectivism, in other words, it no longer mattered to the German Theologians and Scholars in Europe if the resurrection was historically true or not, what mattered was the Christ of faith presented by the church that was proclaimed.

Because of the hammers of biblical criticism that emerged from university professors in Germany, in particular, this lead to a complete deconstruction of the historical narratives themselves, and led to the existential theology of Karl Barth and others that have already been mentioned previously.

There are eight lines of reasoning (**we will summarize only the first three**) that Craig outlines (See pages 272-277) concerning the fact of the empty tomb that is convincing of the resurrection of Jesus. These will be mentioned and discussed in brief as follows: (1) *The Historical Reliability of the Story of Jesus' Burial Supports the*

Empty Tomb. The disciples could not believe in the resurrection if his dead body lay in the tomb. The body of Jesus was missing, it wasn't there. No one is going to believe that Jesus raised from the dead if his body is still there, that is lunacy. In addition to this, the Jewish authorities could simply show anyone the Jesus' dead body to prove that it did not happen, but, again, they were not able to, all they could do is promote the lie that "the disciples stole the body of Jesus." (2) *Paul's testimony Implies the Fact of the Empty Tomb.* In I Corinthians 15 we find a reference to an apparent old tradition in the expression "He was buried" and Paul argues and states clearly that Jesus resurrected, *the significance of this expression is that it implies the fact of an empty tomb.* Although Paul does not directly say that the tomb of Jesus was empty, it is implied. This means that the early belief of his death, burial and resurrection, can't be written off as mere legend and myth that developed over time. (3) *The Empty Tomb Story Is Part of Mark's Source Material and Is Therefore Very Old.* Craig argues that in the writing of the passion story of Jesus, Mark used a source known as Q that is very early. This Q source may have been recorded in Aramaic, which was the language that was spoken by the disciples and Jesus. A German theologian by the name of Rudolf Pesch, argues that "since Paul's traditions concerning the Last Supper (I Cor 11) presuppose the Markan account, that implies that Markan source goes right back to the early years of the Jerusalem fellowship" (Ibid., 274-275).

Moreover, this pre-markan source never mentions this particular high priest by name. This implies that the audience knew all too well WHO this high priest was, which in this case is Caiaphas since he held office from A.D. 18-37. This means then that this pre-markan source would date within seven years of the crucifixion of Christ. This, argues Craig, makes the theory of legend with regards to the tomb being empty one that is just plain falsehood that falls to the ground with no impact whatsoever.

The Conspiracy Theory. This is the biggest

argument that needs to be refuted and put to death once and for all. It is the lie that is put forward that the "disciples stole the body of Jesus." First, on moral grounds this argument is not feasible because the disciples were devout people who wanted to do what was right and submitted to ethical nature of Jesus's teachings. This theory makes the disciples out to be "cheap frauds." Secondly, this theory is psychologically implausible because after the crucifixion the disciples were fearful and went into hiding for the first few days. After this event, argues Craig, the disciples were broken, doubtful, and living in fear, not bold impostors of some cleverly disguised scheme of new religion based upon lies and deceptions. Third, the issue of the disciples sincerity is at stake. These men suffered and were persecuted for what they later believed and proclaimed, they sincerely believed what they preached.

The Apparent Death Theory. Two critical scholars around the 19th century (Heinrich Paulus and Friedrich Schleiermacher) came up with the theory that Jesus' corps never really completely died when he was taken down from the cross, and therefore, when He was in the tomb his body resuscitated to life. Jesus escaped from the tomb and convinced His disciples that He had just risen from the dead. But, once again, this vain theory can be easily refuted on the basis of three important factors: (1) This theory is implausible for physical reasons. Basically, Craig argues that it would be impossible for Jesus to have survived the kind of physical tortures of the crucifixion and entombment. (2) Religious Impossibility. When Jesus resurrected from the dead, as recorded in the gospel records, Jesus was victorious and fully healthy in a glorified body that the disciples touched and felt. If Jesus had merely half died and resurrected after the kind of physical beatings that he received, and therefore the religious implication is that it would be hardly likely that the disciples would be worshiping Jesus as Lord and God when he returned to them in the half-dead condition he would have been in. The testimony of not only the first eyewitnesses that saw Jesus, but, also of the early church, was that Jesus was glorified and rose triumphantly from the grave, not as one who just barely made it out of death and the grave. (3) Lastly, this view holds the position that Jesus basically "tricked" his disciples into believing in His resurrection, and this would not be biographically feasible because it really contracts the ethical sincerity of Jesus' entire ministry, and therefore, this view must be rejected.

The Wrong Tomb Theory. This theory proposed by a scholar by the name of Kirsopp Lake (1907) holds the view that the women that came by the tomb early on Sunday morning were mistaken. The women went to another tomb in the Garden that was empty and stumbled upon a caretaker there who basically said to them, "If you're looking for Jesus of Nazareth He is not here." The women who had this unusual encounter simply fled out of fear, meanwhile, the disciples are having visions of Jesus alive and so the two stories synthesized together formed the historical account of the resurrection. According to Craig

(Ibid., 279) this theory had no following and was basically DEAD on arrival, therefore, no refutation of this view is necessary.

The Facts of the Resurrection Appearances. There are three main lines of evidence that need to be examined about Jesus' resurrection and His appearances. First, *Paul's testimony proves the disciples saw appearances of Jesus.* In I Corinthians chapter 15, Paul gives a list of witnesses of Jesus after the resurrection. Paul claims that Jesus appeared to all 12 of the disciples, we also have individual account of this recorded in John 20:19-20 and Luke 24:36-42, this is probably the most well attested resurrection appearance of Jesus. In addition to this, Paul says that Jesus also appeared to as many as 500 brethren at one time. Craig seems to think that this appearance event happened in Galilee (and not in Jerusalem) in an open area like a hillside of a large crowd that had gathered together to see Jesus. The gospel records do not record this 500 people gathering which is an indicator that it probably did not happen where the Lord was crucified in the city of Jerusalem.

Next, we have the appearance of Jesus to James, the brother of Jesus. This is most convincing to me since James and the other natural brothers of Jesus did not believe He was the Messiah or Prophet or anyone special for that matter during their lifetime, pre-resurrection. The significance of this is that James turns out to be the center leader in the Christian church after Jesus appeared to him, he shows up in the upper room on the Day of Pentecost (See Acts 1:14). In Galatians (See chapter 2:9) we have the account of Paul returning to Jerusalem 14 years later, and he says that there are three pillars in the church there (Peter, John, and James). Later in Acts 21:18 James is mentioned as the sole head of the Jerusalem church and the entire council of the elders there.

James went from being an unsaved and non-believing brother of Jesus, to a follower, and gets promoted to the head of the church in Jerusalem. This to me is one of the greatest NT testimonies not just of the resurrection itself as an independent factual event of history, but also of the mercy of God and that His loving kindness is everlasting, His righteousness prevails and it endures forever. Praise God for second chances and that He truly is the God of mercy.

Finally, we have the conversion of Saul of Tarsus to Paul who turns out to be the theologian *par excellence* and writes two thirds of the books of the NT. This appearance is recorded in Acts 9 and then repeated in later sections of Acts again. Saul was one of the worst enemies of the Lord's new movement that is recorded Acts who was a Rabbi, a Pharisee (an expert at the Jewish Laws of the Torah), a respected Jewish leader, who was responsible for the execution of Christian believers before this conversion. To explain this in modern understanding and vernacular, Saul was a well to do, probably high paid, with much religious-sociological power, in the Jewish community. In other words, Saul had it made where he was at in terms of his socio-religious position of authority and prestige. A man that was highly respected and had everything in this life that a person could want.

However, all of that changed on the road to Damascus (See Acts 9). It is recorded there that Jesus appeared to Saul and temporarily blinded him, Jesus spoke out of a bright light and said, "Saul, Saul, why do you persecute me?" This divine encounter changes Saul's life forever, he left his position with the Jewish religion behind and embraced a life of suffering for himself, beatings, homelessness, ship wrecked, imprisonment, and ultimately died under a Roman Emperor - Paul was beheaded. What can we conclude from such evidence and testimony here? It seems hardly likely that Saul would have changed like this if it were not for a divine encounter with the living Christ. Paul has one of, if not the greatest testimonies in the early church and its development of the message of the death, burial, and resurrection of Jesus.

The second major line of evidence that we have is that, *the Gospel accounts of the resurrection appearances are historically reliable.* This issue here is that the critics would like to argue that these historical narratives given in the records of the disciples are based upon legends, accretions and embellishments, and therefore they are no longer historically informative. However, the problem with this line of argumentation is that there was not enough time that went by from the time of Jesus' resurrection and when the gospels were recorded. Also, with such a strong first-hand eyewitness accounts "and apostolic control of the Jesus tradition -- would act as a restraint upon embellishment and legendary accretion......the demonstrated reliability of the Synoptic evangelists (particularly Luke and Acts) were eternal verification is possible supports their historic credibility" argues Craig (Ibid., 284).

The bottom line concerning this issue is that there simply was not sufficient time for legend to develop and accumulate, therefore, we conclude that the gospel account of the resurrection appearances are historically accurate portraits of the historical details and historical events that certainly, without a doubt, took place as recorded.

The third line of evidence that needs to be examined is that, *the resurrection appearances were physical/spiritual and bodily appearances.* Paul argues that the resurrection will be physical in I Corinthians 15: 42-44 and here Paul describes the differences between the present state of our human bodies, to the future state of the glorified body. Paul describes the earthly body as: mortal, dishonorable, weak, and physical. He describes the resurrected body as: immortal, glorious, powerful, and spiritual.

The implications of Paul's explanations is that the present earthly body will be freed from its slavery and corruption to the sinful nature, and instead in a glorified state, will become empowered by God's spirit and directed by the Spirit in every way. The body will by a physical/spiritual body. The gospels record Jesus eating breakfast with the disciples after He had resurrected.

Charles Craig Lantz, ThD, PhD

The Ultimate Apologetic

Craig has argued that we can know that Christianity is true and authentic because we have the Spirit working on the hearts of humanity. The self-authenticating witness of God's Holy Spirit working, and, that we can show that Christianity is rational based on historical evidence of the resurrection. The resurrection confirms to us that there really is a personal Creator of the universe that does exist and that those who believe in the genuine offer of eternal life through His Son will spend an eternity with God the Father, God the Son, and God the Holy Spirit.

What is the "ULTIMATE APOLOGETIC" that we have? The answer to this question involves two important relationships. First, our relationship to God, and second, our relationship to one another. We find that in Matthew 22:35-40, a rich young Lawyer came to Jesus and wanted to know what is the greatest commandment. Jesus told him to love God with all his heart, his soul, and mind, and to love your neighbor as yourself. These two laws depend all the

Laws and the Prophets. In other words, if we love God and our neighbor as yourself, all is fulfilled as required by the Law of God. Simple right? Not necessarily.

The loving God part probably is the easiest of the the two. Loving God means that He is the total preoccupation in this life. He is everything, He owns us, all that we have is His, and not ours. We give Him the legal right to all that we have and all that we are. We are to live a Christian life totally dedicated to God (Romans 12:1-2) and to be filled with the Holy Spirit (Eph. 5:18). By giving us His very own spirit to indwell us, He is giving part of Himself to us so that we can be empowered to be His followers.

The second aspect of the "Ultimate Apologetic" is loving our neighbor as ourselves. When we love others, we are simply showing them the love that God has shown us. The Apostle John says that God is love. The very essence and nature of who God is is that He is love, therefore, since we know Him we can experience His love in our hearts that is the most powerful force in the whole universe. Paul describes the nature of what this love is found in I Corinthians 13 (this chapter is worth reading and meditation upon everyday for the rest of our lives). This love will empower believers to have servants hearts towards one another. We are exhorted by Paul not to think more highly of ourselves than we ought to, and to serve one another with love (**See Gal. 5:13-14; Phil. 2:3**).

The result of this love for God and love for one another is that it creates an incredible warmth in the body of the community of Christ here on earth. According to Jesus, in John 17:21-23, our love is a sign to the world and to all people that we are His disciples and therefore we serve the world as a testimony that God is real. As the old song goes that we used to sing around the camp fire by the lake during youth group, "they will know we are Christians by our love, yes, they will know we are Christians by our love." How incredibly powerful is that!!!!! The greatest sign and apologetic is not all the evidences presented through logic and reason, but, it is LOVE. When non-believers see our love for each other and our unity they will be drawn to Christ. This will in turn empower them to respond to Christ's offer of salvation.

Personal Testimony. I was shocked when I was a student at WMU back in the early 1980s and met a group of Christians there where I encountered Christ's love by those people that was so powerful that I became convinced that Christianity was true. Never before in my life did I experience the love of God from people like I did in that group of radically committed Christ followers. God used that tight knit bunch of radical Christians to show me God's power to transform my life through the Gospel message which led to rededicating my life to Jesus Christ and 17 years of full-time Christian service. Praise God for His love, and this leads to THE most powerful apologetic--our lives!

Charles Craig Lantz, ThD, PhD

CHAPTER THREE

APOLOGETICS III: MERE CHRISTIANITY[1]

RIGHT AND WRONG AS A CLUE TO THE MEANING
OF THE UNIVERSE

Lewis is a brilliant scholar that emerged during the

World War and conflict between England and attacks by

---

1 "Clive Staples Lewis (1898-1963) was one of the intellectual giants of the twentieth century and arguably one of the most influential writers of his day. He was a Fellow and Tutor in English Literature at Oxford University until 1954, when he was unanimously elected to the Chair of Medieval and Renaissance Literature at Cambridge University, a position he held until his retirement. He wrote more than thirty books, allowing him to reach a vast audience, and his works continue to attract thousands of new readers every year. His most distinguished and popular accomplishments include Mere Christianity, Out of the Silent Planet, The Great Divorce, The Screwtape Letters, and the universally acknowledged classics The Chronicles of Narnia. To date, the Narnia books have sold over 100 million copies and been transformed into three major motion pictures" (Amazon.com, accessed October 29, 2018). This essay is based upon the work of C.S. Lewis, *Mere Christianity*, published by HarperSanFrancisco, Harper Collins Edition, 2001. Lewis is one of the greatest philosophers and apologist of modern times.

Germany, via Hitler's attempted Nazi invasions. He was asked to speak on the radio to encourage citizens and give them hope and meaning to life, and was commissioned to help the common person understand the distinct claims of the Christian Faith, in particular. In Chapter One, Lewis addresses what he calls, The Law of Human Nature. The Law of Human Nature is such that every human being seems to have an inner sense of what is right and wrong. For example, everyone knew that Hitler's killing of the Jews was wrong, it just wasn't right.

Lewis cites several examples to prove his point in explaining the nature of this law. For example, on a basic human level, people want to be treated fairly by their fellow citizens; humans seem to be born with an innate consciousness of moral duty and obligation, explains Lewis. The law would be better defined as, The Law of Human Nature.

A classic example of this Law in human beings, Lewis cites the example of a man who claims to NOT believe in right or wrong, but, then, when someone steals something or a possession of his personal property, then, that same man wants justice, and is not satisfied until the thief is caught. In fact, Lewis says, "we have failed to practice ourselves the kind of human behavior we expect from others" (*Mere Christianity* 2001 7).

Human beings, then, have this innate idea inside of them on how they would like to be treated and how they should behave in a certain way. The Law of Human Nature, or simply put, The Moral Law, is somehow something that is a real thing that must exist outside ourselves, we did not make it up, we were somehow born with an inner knowing of what seems to be good or bad, right or wrong, decent or indecent, moral or immoral. We find that none of us made this Law, but, we find it pressing in upon us.

Nature has its own set of laws that govern it. For example, if one plants an apple seed, eventually one will find that the seed reproduces after its own kind. The Law of Gravity is another example. This Law does not respect person, race, or sex. If a person attempts to jump off a bridge, that person will most certainly fall to the ground and be severely hurt or die, regardless of how good or bad they are as people. The Law of Gravity is there by nature and is no respecter of a person's moral character, or social status, or education status in this world. If you defy the law of gravity as such, you may pay the price of breaking the law.

The question remains, Where did these laws that seem to govern our world come from? Lewis begins to argue that this Law of Human Nature is something that is above and beyond our human nature, and is something that comes from the universe. Now, this tells us something about the universe in which we live, we don't live a universe that has no governing set of laws; we have proven that already. The universe has always been wondered about, and men and women have been trying to figure out "what the universe is" and "how it came into being". These questions have been there for centuries and man has a couple of options here. First, there is the MATERIALIST VIEW.

This is a naturalistic view that gives no real explanation of why the universe is here. They say that the universe has always existed, and that nobody knows why, it just is, all of this life just sort of happened as a fluke, a cosmic act of nature that has no explanation at all, we just accept it that this is all there is to life. This would be described as the EVOLUTIONARY VIEW. This is the humanistic answer as to why we are here. We just evolved out of NOTHING: By random chance of time, space, and matter. This is really an unsatisfactory view that provided us with no hope in this world, no reason to live, except to live for yourself. For the humanist, there is NO SUPERNATURAL POWER behind our universe. However, this is not the religious view, as Lewis sets out to explain.

The fact that man has the answer to this question is really found inside the man. In other words, because man has pressed upon him or her, something that presses them to act in a certain way, is proof that the creation did not just happen. We all seem to be born with the nature that seems to have some knowledge of right and wrong, in addition to the laws we find governing nature. How did these laws get there? The answer is that there must have been an intelligent mind that existed outside of creation,

and that the creator was that mind.

The fact is, argues Lewis that we do not exist on our own; we are under a law, and that somebody or something wants me to behave in a certain way. At this point in the book, Lewis is not arguing for the existence of a Christian God; he is merely arguing and persuading his audience in that there is something in the universe that directs and guides. Lewis writes, "All I have got to is something which is directing the universe, and which appears in me as a law urging me to do right and making me feel responsible and uncomfortable when I do wrong" (Ibid., 25).

At this point, Lewis argues that we have to deal with the fact that there is something or someone out there that created the universe, and also, something or someone which causes us to feel uncomfortable when we do wrong. He is not yet arguing for any kind of Christianity or Judaeo Christian God. He is simple using reason, logic, and the common ground, to get people to understand and realize that there is something else out there that exist outside ourselves.

Lewis points out the fact that we have two bits of evidence of that somebody: 1. The evidence suggests that the being is a great artist; since we have the beauty of the world; 2. The other bit of evidence we have is that there is a Moral Law that this somebody put into our minds that is pressing upon us when we fail or fall short. This is the inside information, a kind of DNA inside us of a kind of morality. "The Being behind the universe is intensely interested in right conduct—in fair play, unselfishness, courage, good faith, and honesty and truthfulness" (Ibid., 30).

It is at this point that Lewis begins to introduce the

concept of Christianity, with all its answers to life's tough questions. Once a person accepts the facts that Lewis has pointed out, Christianity starts to make sense. Hence he says: "It is after you have realized that there is real Moral Law, and a Power behind the law, and that you have broken that law and put yourself wrong with that Power—it is after all this, and not a moment sooner, that Christianity begins to talk. When you know you are sick, you will listen to the doctor" (See pages 31-32). It is now that Lewis begins to introduce to his audience what Christians believe.

WHAT CHRISTIANS BELIEVE

Before Mr. Lewis explains what Christianity believes, he takes the time to explain some rival conceptions of God. By this he means, those views that are held by other religions in the world, Hindus, Platonist, and Stoics, etc., these views do not line up with a Christian view of God. Lewis argues that Christianity is the ONE TRUE religion, and that all others fall short of the truth. As in simple math, there is one right answer among many wrong ones. For example, $1 + 1 = 2$, $4 + 9$ does not $= 10$, you see there are right and wrong views that can be held by other religions of the world.

There are many who believe in a kind of God or gods, as in PANTHEISM. This view holds that God is beyond all good or evil; also, they believe that God animates the universe and that the universe is GOD, so that if the universe did not exist, then neither would God. However, the Christian idea of GOD is quite different. They believe that God created the universe, and that the creation is separate and distinct from the God who made the universe. They are not of the same essence and nature. "A painter is not a picture, and he does not die if his picture is destroyed" writes Lewis (Ibid., 37). We must take the distinction between good and bad seriously. Good and bad are not of the same essence, and are not the same at all. This is what the Christian believes. Lewis argues that when a Pantheist is confronted with cancer or a slum, they will not acknowledge that there is a difference between suffering and someone who does not suffer: the Pantheist will maintain that the suffering is of GOD, meaning that all good and evil are the same; there is no distinction between them.

The Christian, on the other hand, will argue that God made the world and that suffering, sickness, disease, were not part of God's original plan. These things were introduced into the human race, not because God made it that way, but, because people have chosen to hurt one another, and have chosen badly in terms of right and wrong. This, then, introduces another problem for Christianity. Why is there such suffering in the world? How could this be if God made the world perfect? What happened that all this pain and suffering has occurred? Man has been given the power to choose from the beginning. This is the source of all our problems; God did not create a dualistic world where there is one God who is all good, and another equally powerful god who is not all good. This is Greek mythology at this point. This does not satisfy our desire to know that truth and most people don't buy into dualism these days.

The Christian view is that there is a fallen angel, the Devil, who fell from his perfect status with God and became His arch enemy. This evil one was there when man was created and put in the Garden of Eden to be tested. Man was created with the ability to choose and make moral choices. Christianity agrees with dualism only in that there is a war going on, but, not a war going on with equal but opposite forces; it is a REBELLION and a civil war and we are living in the part of the universe that is occupied by an evil outlaw force, named Satan or Lucifer. We live in ENEMY OCCUPIED TERRITORY!!!!! That is what this world is, argues Lewis.

Christians believe that this evil power, called the Devil, has made himself the present Prince of this World. The Devil has been stuck with the notion that this is his planet, and he is at war against the creator. Man was created with the ability to choose evil or good. If man is free to be good, he is also free to choose and be bad. This is the essence of free will. Why did God give us free will? Well, for one thing, He did not want a race of Toy Soldiers who were robots. Introducing free will into the universe give us the power to choose, it enabled evil to be a possible reality, but, it also allowed the possibility of the creator God having a race of beings that freely choose him instead of evil.

Lewis argues that this is the essence of the explaining of why there is good and evil in the universe. Lewis writes, "The happiness which God designs for His higher creatures is the happiness of being freely, voluntarily united to Him and to each other in an ecstasy of love and delight compared with which the most rapturous love between a man and a woman on this earth is mere milk and water. And for that they must be free" (Ibid., 48). For Christianity, God determined that the price that must be paid to have this kind of love between Him and his creatures was the price worth paying that came from free will. So, instead of God creating a toy world, like little children have, where you can pull a string or have a puppet, the creator wanted a world that was real and creatures that freely choose him. The price that had to be paid was creating a world where there was free will.

Lewis uses the analogy between man and an engine. God created man and invented us as a man invented an engine. The mechanical engine will only run on certain fuels, Petrol, and it will not run properly on anything else, like water, milk, soda pop. In a similar fashion, God made man to run good on one thing: HIMSELF. When we fill our lives with other things, other than His Spirit to feed us, we will not end up running right, and we will not achieve happiness.

This is where the Christian Religion comes in. God designed us to be happy when we run on the right fuel. The peace and happiness are by-products of knowing Him and being in a relationship with Him, he fills us up with His love and Spirit. This is the proper order and design. When people live their lives and fill up their gas tanks with other fluids, the motor just chugs along, spits, stutters, and moves slowly. Man has chosen other paths and that is why there is suffering and pain in this world.

Lewis begins to introduce more concepts of Christianity into his lectures. He begins to introduce Jesus the Messiah into the picture. Man was given the choice to sin or not, and, without fail, we have all chosen to rebel. But, the greatness of God is that He provides the solution to His own problem. He makes a provision for our sins to be forgiven, by sending His only Son, Jesus Christ. Now many people are willing to acknowledge that Jesus is a great moral teacher and philosopher, a social scientist that provides man will social and civil solutions of getting along as found in the Sermon on the Mount.

Lewis now is set to make his famous argument: Jesus was either a LIAR, LUNATIC, OR LORD. Lewis is open with his view, that he accepts Jesus as GOD. A God who landed on enemy territory in human form. His flesh veiled his God likeness. "The central Christian belief is that

Christ's death has somehow put us right with God and given us a fresh start. Theories as to how it did this are another matter" argues Lewis (Ibid., 54). The fact is, that we are told that Christ died for our sins, and by doing this, Christ disabled death itself from having a hold on the whole human race. This is the final formula of Christianity and this is what is to be believed and accepted. In Christianity, among other gods, Christ came down from Heaven in the form of a man and lived among us, he eventually was killed and crucified for our sins that restitution with God might be made.

This is the great miracle of Christianity. That God became a man a dwelt amongst us. Lewis urges his hearers to follow God's plan: "Now, today, this moment, is our chance to choose the right side. God is holding back to give us that chance. It will not last forever. We must take it or leave it" (Ibid., 65).

CHRISTIAN BEHAVIOR

When it comes to Christian morality, many have the

idea of a God who doesn't want us to have any fun at all. Some think of God as a grumpy old man who sits up there in heaven watching who is being naughty and nice. To Him, we all are naughty anyways, in terms of His moral character, He is so perfect and beyond our understanding of anything in this world. However, morality is a good thing because it provides a rules and a framework for directions to running the human race. It is sort of like the Stop signs in traffic; they are there for our benefit, not to take away from our happiness, but, to enhance it.

Every rule or moral law of God that has been established is there for so that the human machine can run at its finest without strain or friction; like a cylinder that doesn't properly fire. The rules are all there for the benefit of the human race. Every time someone runs a stop sign, they put at risk others who are following the rules. This is a great analogy of the human race. We are all machines that are designed to run on the right fuel and follow a system which governs the world. Morality was designed by God so that we as humans could perform the best and in unity with the whole human race.

Lewis argues that when we think about morality, "we must think of all three departments: relations between man and man: things inside each man: and relations between man and the power that made him" (Ibid., 75). From here on out, Lewis assumes a Christian point of view, a look at the whole picture as if Christianity were true.

Lewis warns his readers that if they are thinking about becoming a Christian, they are dealing with something that will take on the whole of them. If you want to become a Christian, you must let God be the center of your life. Not just a part of your life, but, He is the central force of it. The central focus of it, the central purpose of your life, and existence. One does not have to become perfect to be a Christ follower, you simply have to have faith and put your trust in Him to save you from your sins; after this, then good works will follow true saving faith. After this, we embrace the great social morality of the New

Testament faith, which is the Gold Rule, "Do unto others as you would have them do unto you." This is the great commandment of Love. If we are to live by that one rule or principle alone, the human race would be greatly transformed.

Also, Christ has given the human race the institution of the Church so that growth can take place amongst believers. We can create a Christian society by following the Golden Rule. Also, Christianity is not religion of people who have no work ethic and expect something for nothing. By and large, there are no passengers or parasites in His Kingdom. All must work and do their part to support themselves.

Lewis addresses the issue of SEXUAL MORALITY which he calls the virtues of chastity. This is the most unpopular of all Christian virtues. Everyone knows that the sexual appetite grows by indulgence, like other appetites of the flesh. Therefore, the Christian must learn how to tame his or her flesh and its appetites. There are numerous sexual perversions that are frightful and hard to cure. But, with Christ and His Word, all things are possible to him who believes. For Christianity, there is nothing evil about sex itself. The creator designed us to have passions for the purposes of procreation, and marital pleasure, between men and women, in a committed/covenant relationship in marriage as the ideal place for this fulfillment. We are human and we will fail, therefore, we must continue to go to God and ask him for strength to overcome our temptations. For some, chastity is not a big deal; it is a preferred way of life; but, not for most. The majority of human beings will engage in some kind of sexual activity.

The laws are there by God so that proper boundaries will enhance our civil relationships with one another. Secular Psychology teaches us that "repressions" are bad and even harmful; therefore, we should indulge our sexual appetites. However, within the confines of the Christian virtue, we as followers of Christ, must deny ourselves and take up our cross. Lewis argues that the sins of the flesh are bad, but they are the least bad of all sins. "All the worst pleasures are purely spiritual: the pleasure of putting other people in the wrong, of bossing and partitioning and spoiling sport, and backbiting, the pleasures of power and hatred" argues Lewis (Ibid., 102-103). We have to overcome the Animal self and the diabolical nature within us that far transcends the mis-virtues of sexual sin. There are far greater sins which one can commit that are horrible abominations to the Lord; how we treat our fellow man is the main issue of Christianity.

This brings up the concept of Christian Marriage. The union between one man and one women is defined as a marriage: the two organisms become one single unity by being joined together as one flesh. The two halves: male and female were to be joined together in pairs, and this is what constitutes marriage in God's eyes. The Christian view is that marriage is for life. Divorce was common in Jesus's day as is ours. It is common because of the hardness of heart, or people falling out of love, and sexual immorality or marital unfaithfulness.

In general, the union between one man and one woman was designed by God to be permanent and for life, till death do us part. Lewis argues that if two people don't believe in permanent marriage, it is perhaps better that they live together until they are ready to make permanent vows that they can keep. The downside of this, though, is that the couple will be viewed as living in sin or sexual immorality. "But one fault is not mended by adding another: chastity is not improved by adding perjury" argues Lewis (Ibid., 107). The reason many couples divorce is that they no longer "feel in-love" and there are many problems with this type of thinking. The state of being in love usually does not last forever, as in the fairy tales. Those intense feelings eventually will wear off. This does not mean that love is not there. Love in this sense, argues Lewis, "is a deep unity, maintained by the will and deliberately strengthened by habit; reinforced by the grace which both partners ask, and receive, from God" (Ibid., 109).

Charles Craig Lantz, ThD, PhD

The fact is that being in love moves the couple to promise fidelity, later, when a deeper love comes into place, and those intense strong feelings subside, and reality kicks in, the quieter love enables them to keep the promise they made to each other. This is the true essence of real Christ like love, agape love...where you would give your life for your best friend that is true love, not Hollywood's version of infatuation. This is the Christian idea of love and marriage.

In Chapters 7-12, Lewis goes into greater details regarding the issues of: Forgiveness, The Sin of Pride, Charity, Hope, and Faith. A brief summary of each concept will follow in order to save space and to keep this paper within proper parameters. First, the issue of forgiveness. Jesus tells us to forgive others in the Lord's Prayer found in Matthew's gospel. "Forgive us our sins as we forgive those that sin against us" said Jesus. This makes it clear that if we want forgiveness we must be willing to forgive others who have sinned against us. The first step in forgiveness is to acknowledge that you have an offense towards someone. Forgiveness is always centered on another person, not a thing; its primary focus is always an individual. There are certain things we can continue to go on hating, but, as far as people, no we can't hate other. This is considered murder in God's eyes. Therefore, forgiveness is not an option for the true Christian.

The second issue that Lewis covers is the Sin of Pride. The sin of pride is self-conceit; it is opposite of humility. Pride is when we exalt ourselves and our ideas above everybody else, even God's. According to Lewis, the central issue or central vice is Pride, which is the utmost evil. All other sins such as sexual vice, anger, drunkenness, greed, and adultery is feeble compared to the sin of pride. This is the sin that Lucifer committed and became the Devil since his fall from grace in heaven.

Lewis argues, "it was through Pride that the devil became the devil: Pride leads to every other vice: it is the complete anti-God state of mind" (Ibid., 122). These are indeed strong words that describe this sin. Proud people look down on others and causes them to think more highly of themselves than they should. Jesus said that the meek or humble will inherit the earth. God resists the proud but gives grace to the humble. When we are prideful, we do not say we are sorry to others and refuse to repent of our sins to God. This is a terrible sin.

The third is that of Charity. The word Charity means 'love in the Christian sense'. Love in this sense does not necessarily mean an emotion. "It is a state not of the feelings but of the will; that state of the will which we have naturally about ourselves, and must learn to have about other people" writes Lewis (Ibid., 129). There is a sharp distinction between loving someone and liking them. We as Christians do not have to like everybody the same. We are commanded to Love one another the way God loves us.

Many people love others based on the fact that others treat them kind and good. We are commanded to love our enemies and pray for those who persecute us.

Lewis argues that a "worldly" man will like certain people and be kind and good to them in a charitable way. But, for the true Christian, we are to treat everyone kindly. We find that as time goes on he/she is liking more and more people, and finds that they are kind to people who don't deserve it. This is real Love. The forces of good and evil are at work in the hearts of people.

Love and hate are powerful and produce powerful emotions. Those that hate are crueler, and the more you hate, the crueler you become. It ends up being a vicious cycle that only the power of Christ's love can break. The great truth about God's love for us is that it does not come and go according to His feelings. His love for us is not "worried by our sins, or our indifference; and, therefore, it is quite relentless in its determination that we shall be cured of those sins, at whatever cost to us, at whatever cost to Him" says Lewis.

The next issue that Lewis addresses is that of HOPE. We have hope and in a theological sense it is a virtue. We have an eschatological hope in that we look forward to the eternal world. It is a form of escapism and wishful thinking; thinking of Heaven and a better place to live than on earth. We are exhorted to focus on heaven as our home. We are not to store up for ourselves treasures on earth where moth and rust destroy, said Jesus. Hope is in our hearts daily because we know that there is a divine being out there beyond this world we can see who is governing all things, and watching over us at all time.

The hope of Jesus gives us a reason to want to keep living and a long term perspective on life. The follower of Jesus realizes that we will live forever and ever, with Christ in our eternal state of blessedness. Earth is our temporary home and Heaven is our destiny. This is proper hope that we have daily.

The final issue discussed by Lewis is that of faith. In a simple sense, faith simply means belief—accepting and regarding as true the essential doctrines of Christianity. This is faith. But, for many of us, the real battle is between faith and human reason. Our human moods may change, but, our faith is not based upon how we feel that day. Our faith is based upon a true conviction that God raised Jesus from the dead. The doctrines of Christ and His resurrection, do not change based upon how we feel. We have to learn to set aside the moodiness of Christianity and settle on the facts, and let those facts become the bedrock of our faith. Lewis argues that this "is why daily prayers and religious readings and church-going are necessary parts of the Christian life. We have to be continually reminded of what we believe. Neither this belief nor any other will automatically remain alive in the mind. It must be fed" (Ibid., 141). Faith comes from hearing the Word of Christ, writes Paul in Romans 10:17.

Our faith must be fed the Word of God or the sincere milk of the word in order to grow. Just as a plant can wither away if it does not get the proper sunlight and water, so to our faith can wither away, and, as a result of this. Many souls have drifted away from the faith, or they have been talked out of their belief in Christ because trials. And temptations came, and the Word was stolen from their hearts. As a Christian grows in the faith in God, they develop a deeper trust in Him. There are times in life when we must leave it all to Him, and we must put all our hope and trust in Christ. "To trust Him means, of course, trying to do all that he says. There would be no sense in saying you trusted a person if you would not take his advice" urges Lewis (Ibid., 147). If we believe in Christ, we will trust, obey, and follow Him every day of our lives.

Moreover, if we have true faith we will not continue living a sinful life. We will repent and follow Christ's teachings. True faith is going to require that we take notice of the things that Christ taught His disciples in His Word, the Bible. We can work out our salvation with fear and trembling. For most people, writes Lewis, "Christianity seems at the first to be all about morality, all about duties and rules and guilt and virtue, yet it leads you on, out of all that, into something beyond" (Ibid., 149). This is the essence of true saving faith.

THE FIRST STEPS IN THE DOCTRINE OF THE

TRINITY

This is the last section of the book, *Mere Christianity*, which deals now with the subject of theology itself. The word "theology" means the scientific study of God. Therefore, we study God and come to concrete definitions of His nature, character, and His divine person-hood. Theology, in a sense, is like a road map. The doctrines about God are like the map. As Lewis says, "But that map is based on the experience of hundreds of people who really were in touch with God—experiences compared with which any thrills or pious feelings you and I are likely to get on our own are very elementary and very confused" (Ibid., 154).

Basically, without a road map when traveling, it is easy for one to get lost. In a similar way, we are traveling on the path of life by faith and going to a certain destination called "Heaven" which to get there we need definition and guidance. Theology helps us know the truth from errors; and, there are plenty of errors that people unknowingly believe. Theology will provide the proper grounding of our faith so that we are not led astray from the faith. The fact is, argues Lewis, is that "Christianity claims to be telling us about another world, about something behind the world we can touch and hear and see. You may think the claim false, but if it were true, what it tells us would be bound to be difficult—at least as difficult as modern physics, and for the same reason" (Ibid., 156).

Lewis starts with a theological discussion about the fact that we are "Sons" of God. What does this mean? It means that God brought us into existence and loves and looks after us as a father would to his son. But we become "sons" when we place our faith in His Son, Jesus Christ. This brings us to the very center of theology: **Christ is the Son of God 'begotten, not created' and 'begotten by His Father before all worlds'.** Theology raises the distinction between God making something, and God begetting something. When God makes man, he made man as man, and not as God. However, when God begat his Son, He begat God. "What God creates is not God; just as what man makes is not man" Argues Lewis. Everything that God made is somehow in His likeness. God created man in His image and likeness, but, we are NOT God in nature.

Lewis defines the terms "Bios" and "Zoe." God created nature and natural things; nature in the form of air, water, and food is 'Bios.' The Spiritual life by which God created the entire universe was done by a 'Zoe.' So, God created man out of *Bios* and then when man believes he or she is brought into the life force of God called *Zoe.* This divine change takes a man or women from being a statue or carved stone, into being a real man or woman. "And that is precisely what Christianity is about. This world is a great sculptor's shop. We are the statues and there is a rumor going round the shop that some of us are someday going to come to life" says Lewis (Ibid., 159).

We now come to the subject of the Trinity. This is a

complex subject and one of which has been debated much in the days of the early Church. The creator God is ONE being yet He has clearly revealed himself as three distinct persons: Father, Son, and Holy Spirit. This is a difficult concept for us to understand. But let's see if we can illustrate this concept of the trinity. The substance of water, H2O, can come in the form of liquid, steam, or ice. The essence is the same, but, it can manifest in three separate and distinct ways to us. Another difficult concept about God is that he is outside of time and space as we know it. This eternal being does not live inside time and space as we do; this is how He is able to manage the affairs of man. He sees everything from an "Eternal Now" moment.

We, therefore, experience time, but, He is the author of time. He is the Alpha and Omega, the beginning and the end all at once. This is how God as Father can be one with the Son, and the Holy Spirit, all at once. This is how the Father can answer millions of individual prayers all at once. Lewis explains this concept like this: "His life does not consists of moments following one another....He has all eternity in which to listen to the split second of prayer put up by a pilot as his plane crashes in flames" (Ibid., 167). The beautiful thing about God is that He has infinite amount of attention He can spare of us as individuals. He does not have to deal with us as one big mass of people at such and such a moment in time. We are as much alone with Him as if we are the only being he created. When Jesus died for us, he died for us individually, just as much as if we had been the only ones in the world for which He died. Because of this concept of eternity, we can say with confidence that Christ died for all of our sins, past, present, and future. He loves us that much.

That is what makes the Christian story so special and unique from all other religions of the world. This is the whole offer of Christianity: that we can let God into our lives so that we can share in the life of Christ while on earth. "If we share in this kind of life we also shall be sons of God. We shall love the Father as He does and the Holy

Ghost will arise in us" writes Lewis (Ibid., 177). Christ came to spread a good infection in us of His divine nature. For, writes Lewis, "Every Christian is to become a little Christ. The whole purpose of becoming a Christian is simply nothing else" (Ibid., 177).

God the Father has sent His Son, Jesus Christ, to be with us and live inside of us. We do not merely conform externally to rules and regulations of God's moral laws. The realness of Christianity is that Christ the Son of God is at our side. He has a goal to turn us into the image of Himself; to become as He is in nature. "He is beginning, so to speak, to 'inject' His kind of life and thought, His Zoe, into you; beginning to turn the tin soldier into a live man. The part of you that does not like it is the part that is still tin." (Ibid., 189). But as time goes on, the tin man becomes more and more real and changes from being a tin toy soldier into a living being.

Christ is the 'good infection' for humanity. We are His carriers to pass on the infection to other by coming into contact with others and passing on the good infection of Christ to others who do not know Him, this is the God ordained method of slowing transforming the human race into a race of living beings that are little Christ's. This goal of becoming little Christ's was the commission of the Church. The Church is not really a physical building as such, but, rather, it is a body of believers that represent Christ to the world. Lewis argues that the Church exists for nothing else but that to draw men to himself and to make them little Christ's. "If they are not doing that, all the cathedrals, clergy, missions, sermons, even the Bible itself, are simply a waste of time. God became man for no other purpose" argues Lewis (Ibid., 199). As a matter of fact, the Bible says that the whole world and universe was made for Christ and that everything is gathered together into him. This is the great purpose of God in creation.

As we come to the close of the book, *Mere Christianity*, Lewis also points out that there is a "counting the cost" of following our Lord. In the Sermon on the

Mount Christ says "be perfect". Lewis argues that Christ's purpose is to make us perfect in every way. Lewis says that the Lord is like a Dentist, in that, if you give him an inch, he will take a mile. Once you call on the Lord to get help for this or for that, He never stops working on you. His goal is for us to be like little Christ's. This means that the Lord will continually put us in situation in our lives that might cause us to be uncomfortable, but, in that, He is accomplishing His work in us: to make us more like Jesus Christ.

You see, when the Father spoke and said, "This is my beloved son with whom I am well pleased" this is the same goal that the Father has for all who are follower of Him. We may never reach a state of sinless perfection, but, each time we fall or fail, He is there to pick us up again. He is a loving Father that expects us to be perfect in every way, argues Lewis.

So, "the question is now what we intended ourselves to be, but what he intended us to be when He made us. He is the inventor, we are only the machine. He is the painter, we are only the picture" writes Lewis (Ibid., 203). His plans are bigger than ours, and we are destined to be in the Father's house. He is building a big palace and one day will be taken home to live with Jesus in the Father's house in Heaven. God can take a life that has been ruined by drugs, sex, money, you name it, and He can redeem us from sickness, sin, and disease.

He can take the filthiest of sinners and make him or her whole again, and beautiful on the inside and out. He is the potter and we are the clay, this is the beauty of God's way of doing things. We don't always understand why we are going through what we are experiencing in life, but, the Father is at work in our hearts and developing Christ-likeness in our souls.

As we come to the conclusion of this book, it needs to be said that Christianity is not a "hard religion." What Lewis means by this is that, it is only hard if we are unyielding to Him and live our lives as if they are our own. We have been bought with a price, and our life does not belong to ourselves to do with as we wish. God did not become a man so that we could become nicer people. He became a man so that we could become a "new" kind of race.

Let us hear the words of Lewis and take them to heart: "Give up yourself, and you will find your real self. Love your life and you will save it. Submit to death, death of your ambitions and favorite wishes every day and death of your whole body in the end: submit with every fiber of your being, and you will find eternal life...look for Christ and you will find Him, and with Him everything else thrown in" (Ibid., 226-227).

SELECTED BIBLIOGRAPHY

Craig, William Lane. 1994. *REASONABLE FAITH: CHRISTIAN TRUTH AND APOLOGETICS.* ILLINOIS: Crossway Books.

Geisler, Norman L. 2006. *Christian Apologetics.* Grand Rapids: Baker Books.

Groothuis, Douglas. 2011. *Christian Apologetics: A Comprehensive Case for Biblical Faith.* Illinois: Intervarsity press.

Lewis, C.S. 1980. *Mere Christianity.* New York: Harper Collins Publishers.

McDowell, Josh. 1993. *The Best Of Josh McDowell: A Ready Defense.* Tennessee: Thomas Nelson Publishers.

McDowell, Josh, & McDowell, Sean. 2017. *EVIDENCE THAT DEMANDS A VERDICT: LIFE-CHANGING TRUTH FOR A SKEPTICAL WORLD.* Tennessee: Thomas Nelson Publishers.

Moreland, J.P., and Craig, William Lane. 2003. *Philosophical Foundations For a Christian Worldview.* Illinois: Intervarsity Press.

Price, Randall. 2007. *Searching for the Original Bible.* Eugene: Harvest House.

Price, Randall. 1996. *SECRETS OF THE DEAD SEA SCROLLS.* Oregon: Harvest House Publishers.

Charles Craig Lantz, ThD, PhD

Wallace, Daniel. 2011. *The Reliability of the New Testament: Bart Ehrman and Daniel Wallace in Dialogue.* Minneapolis, MN: Fortress Press.

Books by Charles Craig Lantz, Th.D, Ph.D.

Available to order at Amazon.com

A Biblical Survey of the Old Testament:

A Brief and Concise Guide to Understanding the Old Testament

A Biblical Survey of the New Testament:

A Concise Handbook on the New Testament Canonical Books

Christian Counseling: An Introduction

A Concise Guide for Ministers and Christian Workers in the Field of
Christian Counseling

CHURCH LAW:

A Concise Legal Handbook for Ministers, Pastors, and Church Leaders

Ethics:

A Concise Handbook on Contemporary Issues

Hermeneutics:

The Science and Art of Biblical Interpretation

A Brief and Concise Handbook on How to Interpret the Bible

Charles Craig Lantz, ThD, PhD

Philosophy of Religion:

An Examination of the Arguments for the Existence of God, and

the Problem of Evil

Systematic Theology:

A Brief and Concise Handbook

The Role of Faith and Grace in the Life and Theology of

Dietrich Bonhoeffer:

Pastor, Theologian, Prophet, and Martyr

World Religions:

An Investigation of the Origins, Nature, and Doctrines of

Seven Major World Religions

A Brief and Concise Handbook on Seven non-Christian Religions

The Biblical Studies Synopsis Research Project:

A Synopsis Study of All 66 Canonical Books of the Holy Bible, 28

Biblical Expository Sermon Outlines, The Prophets of Israel, and,

The Synoptic Gospel Problem

Charles Craig Lantz, ThD, PhD

828 Questions and Statement Answered:

Five Major Subjects Examined with Questions and Statements

Answered in Systematic Theology, Biblical Theology,

Eschatology, The Book of Revelation, and Hermeneutics

Why I am NOT a King James ONLY advocate:

An Apologetic for the Faith

Printed in Great Britain
by Amazon